DAYDREAMS & NIGHTMARES

A NATION DIVIDED:
STUDIES IN THE CIVIL WAR ERA
Orville Vernon Burton and Elizabeth R. Varon, *Editors*

Daydreams
&Nightmares

A Virginia Family Faces Secession and War

Brent Tarter

University of Virginia Press

CHARLOTTESVILLE AND LONDON

University of Virginia Press
© 2015 by the Rector and Visitors of the University of Virginia
All rights reserved
Printed in the United States of America on acid-free paper
First published 2015

ISBN 978-0-8139-3709-0 (cloth)
ISBN 978-0-8139-3710-6 (ebook)

9 8 7 6 5 4 3 2 1

Library of Congress Cataloging-in-Publication Data is available from the
Library of Congress.

Illustrations not otherwise credited are from the Berlin-Martz Family Papers,
Library of Virginia.

Contents

Preface

Every folder, box of manuscripts, bound volume of historic records, and reel of microfilm in every research library contains stories about people. This story comes in large part from a reel of microfilm of the Berlin-Martz Family Papers in the Library of Virginia. It is the story of George William Berlin and Susan Miranda Holt Berlin, of Buckhannon, in Upshur County, Virginia, one of the counties that in 1863 became part of West Virginia. The story begins in February 1861, when he traveled to Richmond to serve in the state convention called to deal with the secession crisis. It ends after October 1862, when they were reunited after being twice separated by political and military crises.

This true story is derived in large part from the incomplete file of surviving letters that they exchanged during their separations. Because there is nothing so valuable for trying to understand how past events affected people as the words of the people who lived through the events, the narrative contains extended excerpts from their letters. The words that they wrote and the ways that they described their experiences and their hopes and fears give valuable insights into their beliefs and emotions. Through their letters, they told their stories to each other, and to a large extent the letters tell their stories to us, too. Other family papers, public records, and the letters and diaries of other people enrich the context and fill in some of the gaps, particularly with respect to the political choices that George Berlin faced in 1861, choices that had dramatic consequences for him and his family.

The story of George and Susan Berlin and their family is of comparatively ordinary white mountain Southerners and what they did on the eve of the Civil War and during its first year and a half. The Berlins were more prosperous than most of their neighbors, but they were not wealthy. He was an aspiring attorney living in a town, not a great planter, not an independent small farmer, not a poor laboring man. In that, the Berlins were not stereotypical white Southerners, but during the middle decades of the nineteenth century professional men in small Southern towns were an increasingly numerous and important class of white Southerners. George and Susan Berlin owned no slaves, but they hired an enslaved man and young white girls or enslaved women to assist with

Virginia places that played a part in the lives of George and Susan Berlin in 1861–62. (Map by Chris Harrison)

work in the garden and at household labor, setting them just a notch above most of their neighbors and contemporaries in the mountains of northwestern Virginia and involving them personally in the economy of slavery. The Berlins may also have been better educated than some of their neighbors, and they had traveled back and forth across the mountains to eastern Virginia often enough that they may have had a wider acquaintance than their neighbors with the people and geography of western Virginia.

In 1861 George and Susan Berlin lived in a large, loose family group consisting of their five children; his brother and her sister, who were married to each other, had a large number of children, and also resided in Buckhannon; and also her parents and several brothers and sisters, who lived in nearby Philippi, in Barbour County, or sometimes with them. The story of George and Susan Berlin is therefore, in part, also a story of their extended family. In 1861 they and millions of other Americans got caught up in very remarkable events. Their story is about how extraordinary events shaped the lives of comparatively ordinary people and how they acted in those new circumstances.

Members of the Berlin family were not wholly consumed by the secession crisis and the war even as it directly altered their lives. They continued to take care of their own personal and family affairs early in 1861 as if the Civil War was not going to happen. The ordinary business of earning a living, bringing up their children, and helping their in-laws remained at the center of their attentions. Those activities and connections were the most important factors that governed how they lived their lives. The secession of Virginia and the resulting war changed the context in which they tried to continue to live their lives. Extraordinary events of extraordinary times then disrupted the ordinary lives of rather ordinary people.

Dramatic historic events happen in a context that is different for every person involved. The story of the Berlins is unique, but their story shares important large themes with the stories of millions of other Americans and their families who had their own unique experiences during those same extraordinary times. It is a very personal story, which is why it is important to read their words carefully and at length. How they wrote, and what they wrote, are both important. Consequently, I have employed a narrative prose style adapted to their speaking and writing styles to help readers into and out of George and Susan Berlin's words and thoughts, the better to understand what the extraordinary events meant to them.

I have quoted their letters as nearly *verbatim ac litteratim* as possible, including the many misspellings, run-on sentences, and other imperfections that their letters include. In some instances it is difficult to determine whether the writer intended a capital or lowercase letter, and in those instances I have rendered the characters in lowercase type except at the beginnings of sentences. Both writers added postscripts or made additions to their letters, sometimes squeezing text into narrow margins or writing them on attached slips of paper. Unless it is clear from the context or by the presence of asterisks or carets in the originals, I have interpreted those additions as postscripts.

The letters have never before been published, and with a few exceptions no other historian has used them. My colleagues and I at the Library of Virginia reproduced one letter from George Berlin in our *Union or Secession: Virginians Decide* website in 2010; Clarence E. May had access to the papers and mentioned them in passing in his *Life under Four Flags in the North River Basin of Virginia* (1976); and my friend and colleague Daphne S. Gentry used them to prepare the entry on George W. Berlin for volume one of the *Dictionary of Virginia Biography* (1998), of which she was an assistant editor before her retirement and subsequent death in 2007.

She tracked down the family papers and brought them to the attention of archivists at the Library of Virginia, who arranged for the collection to be microfilmed and preserved as the Berlin-Martz Family Papers, Acc. 36271, Miscellaneous Microfilm reel 2051 in the Library of Virginia in Richmond.

For their valuable advice and assistance, I particularly thank Noel Tenney, Amy Murrell Taylor, Melvin P. Ely, John G. Deal, Dan Crofts, Michael B. Chesson, William W. Blair, and the late Daphne Gentry.

DAYDREAMS & NIGHTMARES

1 | Daydreams

John Tyler was midway through a very long speech in Richmond, Virginia, at one o'clock on the afternoon of March 14, 1861. Twenty years earlier Tyler had been president of the United States, and more recently he had been president of a hopefully styled Peace Conference that met in Washington, D.C., but he was not talking about peace, now. John Tyler was talking about the breaking up of the nation. Seven lower South slave states had seceded from the United States, and he told delegates from every county in Virginia, assembled in Richmond to deal with the secession crisis, about how and why the nation might soon break apart the rest of the way. He had talked on the previous day about differences between the Southern states, where slavery was legal and flourishing, and the Northern states, where slavery was not legal and the population was increasingly hostile to the South's peculiar institution. John Tyler had talked for a long time on the previous day, and now he was talking again, his speech consuming a large part of one afternoon and more than two hours of the next.

Old and feeble, now, his voice weak and often inaudible, John Tyler nevertheless talked and talked and talked. He told the other delegates that the Peace Conference had failed to offer enough inducements to the politicians in the states that had already seceded to bring them back into the Union. At the same time, political leaders in the free states feared that it yielded too much to the slave states. Tyler had already explained that owners of enslaved laborers could no longer feel secure in taking their slave property into the western territories. Now he reported that the compromise proposals that came from the conference over which he had presided threatened to reduce, rather than to protect, slaveholders' rights. Today, a month after the convention began, he talked about whether proposals to compromise the differences between the sections of the nation were genuine and hopeful or whether slave owners in the Southern states would be forced to yield to a Northern majority that seemed bent on preventing the spread of slavery into the western territories. That would bottle up slavery where it then existed, and the expense of feeding the surplus of laborers might actually destroy the institution that white Southerners were trying to preserve.

John Tyler was gloomy. Voters in the states without slavery had recently elected a president who made no secret of his distaste for slavery, the first such president in the country's history, elected on a campaign platform that specifically demanded that slavery be confined within its existing borders. That president, Abraham Lincoln, had been inaugurated only ten days earlier. Those same voters, Tyler and his audience very well knew, might some day try to abolish slavery, the foundation stone of the South's whole economy and society. John Tyler was very gloomy.[1]

A newspaper reporter took down Tyler's words in Richmond's Mechanic's Institute, where the convention was temporarily meeting while the General Assembly occupied the legislative chamber in the nearby Capitol. Tyler later wrote out his report so that the whole speech, both days of it, could be printed in the newspapers. While he spoke, other convention delegates and ladies and gentlemen in the gallery strained to hear his words, not willing to wait for the published version, not wanting to miss the high drama of a former president of the United States talking about the very preservation of the nation. Some of them probably lost the thread of his argument or missed some of what he said. John Tyler's voice was weak and often inaudible.

One of the delegates lost the train of argument entirely. He began to daydream, to think about his wife and children back home. George William Berlin, age thirty-six,[2] had left them in the town of Buckhannon, in Upshur County, on the western slopes of the Allegheny Mountains. He missed his wife and his five little children, the eldest twelve, the youngest three.[3] As John Tyler talked on and on and the background noise that filtered into the room from outdoors drowned out the old man's feeble voice, Berlin began to daydream about his home and family. He finally gave up trying to follow what Tyler was saying and pulled out a sheet of paper on which he had written several paragraphs to his wife early that morning before the convention resumed its meetings at noon.[4]

He had written then about how the night before he and another delegate, who happened to be a brother-in-law of his wife's brother, had sat up comparing notes on the beauties and excellencies of their wives. Both men missed their wives and families, and Berlin, at least, had already begun to regret that he had allowed himself to be elected to the convention and separated from them by too many miles and for too many weeks. He had finally received a letter from his wife, Susan Miranda Holt Berlin, who was a year or two younger than he, so he had learned a few days earlier that the mail had been robbed between Buckhannon and Clarksburg and that his wife's letters, together with many others, had been destroyed or thrown to the wind after the thief did not find any money enclosed in them.[5] He read his wife's words of love and her repeated expressions of hope that he would return home safely and soon. It was one o'clock, and the convention had been meeting for an hour. John Tyler had been talking for most of that time.

George Berlin inked his pen and began to write: "Hall of the Convention 1 Oclock. P.M. As Ex. President John Tyler is now speaking but so low in consequence of his age & febleness that I can not hear him, I will add that peace prospects are rapidly improving & Union feelings becoming stronger! & we now believe that harmony will soon prevail again in our Country." Berlin had not been able to hear clearly, or his daydreaming had distracted him. He had evidently not been following Tyler's speech closely enough to grasp the implications of what the former president was saying. Tyler was reciting a dreary list of capital failures in the nation's most recent attempt to reach a compromise that would undo what extremists in the North and South had done. Seven states had seceded and organized the Confederate States of America. Such a

George William Berlin and Susan Miranda Holt Berlin (inset, in the only surviving photograph of her, perhaps the one she sent to him in January of 1862).

thing was so difficult for Berlin and for hundreds of thousands of other Americans to imagine that in spite of the deep forebodings that ruined their digestions and their sleep, in spite of the very words to which they were listening as John Tyler talked on and on, in spite of everything, they could not believe that the United States would permanently fracture or plunge itself into civil war. The unreality of what they were hearing may have made men like Berlin tone deaf to the implications of Tyler's words.

While Tyler talked, Berlin worried about whether he would get home in time to sow seeds in his vegetable garden, to plant some fruit trees, to see whether any of his neighbors had pilfered from the stacks of stone, brick, and lumber with which he was hoping to build a new and larger house for his family. He missed his family more and more every day as the convention dragged on and on. He thought about them often, wondering whether they were healthy and safe. He had not heard anything about them for more than a month after he had left home to attend the convention. Lack of news from and about his wife and children made Berlin worry even more. A few days earlier he wrote to instruct his wife to place the key of the upper room in the inside lock so that if fire broke out nobody would be trapped. A fire in Richmond had reminded him that the key was where he usually kept it when he was at home, not where his wife and children, who relied on him for protection, would be able to find it.[6]

That day, as on other days, even as Berlin sat in his seat trying to listen to the speakers in the convention, he daydreamed about his family in Buckhannon. It was a busy town in a pretty place, taking its name from the little Buckhannon River, which, flowing north out of the mountains, had found or made a wide and relatively flat valley among the hills as it tumbled down toward the Ohio. The first settlers a century earlier had recognized a good town site when they saw it and put down their roots on the southwest side of a sharp right-hand bend in the river. By western Virginia standards in 1861 the town was fairly large, especially if compared with the little villages that dotted Upshur County's forested hills and narrow valleys. Buckhannon had several hundred inhabitants, mostly clustered near the new courthouse or spread out along the river.

Hall of the Convention 1 Oclock. P. M.

As Ex. President - John Tyler is now speaking but so low in consequence of his age & feebleness that I can not hear him. I will add that peace prospects are rapidly improving, & Union feelings becoming stronger, & we now believe that harmony will soon prevaile again in our Country

I recd a letter from Bro. F. today by the hands of Mr Byrne who has just returned from the oil wells, I fear that he will involve himself by risking too much upon uncertainties, the temptation is very great it is true. But as Mr Byrne says that no oil has yet been found off of Rathbones land I should invest very cautiously until some one had been successful on adjoining lands, But I hope & pray that Brother may be successful & make a fortune, But if I were in his place I would act as agent for some of the Companys there as they pay high wages to good agents — I will write to him to-night, write soon. I look for a letter from you this evening & hope I shall not be disappointed, I recd a very kind & satisfactory letter from Maria on yesterday for which I thank her very much Affectionately

Yours
G. W. Berlin

The town had the usual compliment of merchants, cobblers, tinkers, blacksmiths, and school teachers, a couple of hotels that gave lodging to unmarried professional men, and a small number of attorneys to help keep track of all the land transactions and straighten out the many conflicts that a century of speculation and overlapping claims had produced.

George Berlin was one of the attorneys. He had built or remodeled a house there in 1852,[7] but it may have been damaged in a fire that destroyed a good deal of the town in October 1855.[8] Now, he planned to build a proper new brick residence suitable for the successful young professional gentleman that he had become. Berlin owned four and a half acres of land on the opposite bank of the Buckhannon River in a big horseshoe bend that the river made, just as if it were lazily flowing through a flat delta and not through a mountain valley. A millrace closed the open end of the horseshoe, leaving the center entirely surrounded by water. Locals called it (and still call it) the island. Berlin had purchased a quantity of brick, stone, and lumber and stockpiled them there, intending to build a large residence for his family in the warm months of 1861.

As an attorney at law living in a bustling town, George Berlin was part of an increasingly numerous and important class of nineteenth-century Virginians. Professional men such as attorneys, physicians, clergymen, teachers, and merchants in Virginia's towns and cities were the new class of civic leaders, replacing the tobacco planters who had dominated society and government during most of the previous two and a half centuries. In their towns and cities, the professional men and their families cultivated civic values, sang popular songs to the accompaniment of pianos in their parlors, read the latest national periodicals, and formed themselves into what elsewhere and in larger American cities would have been regarded as an emerging bourgeois community. Their

Facing page: Last page of George Berlin's letter to Susan Berlin, March 14, 1861.

Pages following: Buckhannon, Upshur County, drawing by Lewis Miller, 1871. (Lewis Miller Drawing Book, 1856–71, Mss5:10 M6155:1, Virginia Historical Society)

2 5

Leffner's house

church

Buckhannon, 2

Paid A visit In May . 6 2

at Minter, Miller and St

art house

Church

...r County, West Virginia,
...d 8th 1869, then of to Sandy run,
...the 24th day of may.

perspectives and values were much the same as the perspectives and values of urban Americans elsewhere. They read the same national periodicals, dressed in essentially the same styles, and founded and supported temperance societies, religious organizations, and social service clubs. Even if they did not all recognize the fact, they were the emerging new leaders of Virginia.[9] At the convention that George Berlin attended early in 1861, almost exactly two-thirds of the delegates were or had been practicing attorneys. The same had been the case in the state's most recent constitutional convention in 1850–51,[10] just as the same was the case in nearly every other American state at that time.

However difficult to imagine the possibility of disunion had been before the winter of 1860–61, it had become reality, and it had brought Berlin and 151 other Virginia men to Richmond for the convention. Opponents of secession, Berlin among them, held a large majority of the seats in the convention, and they hoped that once more, as in the past, some wise men could contrive a means of patching up the differences. It had happened before, and it could happen again. Back in 1820, just a few years before Berlin was born in Pennsylvania, Henry Clay and other members of Congress had compromised the differences that arose when Missouri applied for statehood, threatening to alter the national political balance between the states with slavery and the states without slavery. For the next thirty years the country thrived and grew. In spite of clearly widening differences between the region with slavery and the region without slavery, their differences did not tear the country apart. Indeed, in some respects the rapidly expanding cotton and sugar plantations of the South contributed significantly to the industrial and economic growth of the North and the whole nation. Compromise had been possible before, and compromise had worked.

Compromise had worked again in 1850 when Berlin was a young attorney in the mountains of northwestern Virginia. He had grown up in Pennsylvania and moved to Ohio, traveled as far west as the Mississippi River,[11] and then returned to the east to teach school in Augusta County, Virginia. Quickly growing disillusioned with teaching, he moved into Staunton, where he and his brother Frederick Berlin studied law with a distinguished attorney, Lucas P. Thompson, and married sisters.[12] Frederick Berlin married Maria F. Holt in 1844,[13] and George Berlin married Susan Miranda Holt in 1846.[14] They were two of the six daughters of Thomas Holt and Minerva Graham Holt, who lived on a farm in the northern part of Augusta County. Susan Holt was about twenty when they married, George Berlin twenty-one. He was admitted to the bar early in 1846[15] and not long thereafter opened an office in the town of Beverly in the mountains of western Virginia. By the summer of 1850 when a new sectional crisis arose, he had moved a few miles west to Buckhannon.[16] George Berlin became an officer of and speaker for the Sons of Temperance; and his sister Catherine Berlin lived there, too, and taught school before she married.[17]

Berlin was a young man on the way up the social and professional ladders in 1850 when the nation faced another crisis about the admission of new western states following the war with Mexico and the rapid movement of thousands of Americans into the southwest and the Great Plains. Owners of enslaved people in the South believed that they had a right to take their slave property into the new western territories, where many of them expected to create new western slave states; but opponents of slavery in the North objected and tried to prohibit the spread of slavery into and across the Great Plains and to prevent the creation of more slave states. As before, Henry Clay and talented national statesmen had fashioned a compromise, one that did not entirely satisfy anybody, but one that satisfied enough people well enough that the country held together again.

Now, though, there was no Henry Clay. He had been dead for nine years. His death might have seemed to symbolize or foreshadow the end of nation-saving compromises. If the Great Compromiser—for that was the honorable title he earned in twice saving the nation—was dead, did that mean that hope of compromise was also dead? Virginians in Clay's native state of Virginia, as well as most other Americans, hoped not. Virginia women who had been ardent admirers of Clay had raised a private subscription to erect a splendid, life-sized marble statue of Clay on the grounds of the Capitol in Richmond in 1860. The statue of Clay shared conspicuous place with another statue of an even greater patriot. The other statue was a spectacular greater-than-life-sized bronze equestrian figure of George Washington, the founder of the nation of which Clay was the savior. Nobody could mistake the symbolic pairing of those two figures. The dedication ceremonies of the Washington statue in 1858 and of the Clay statue in 1860 had been widely reported in the country's newspapers and emphasized the founding and the preservation of the nation in an age of increasing sectional tension.[18]

Berlin knew precisely what the two statues symbolized and what generations before him had done in times of crisis. He had himself prospered after the last, great compromise. In 1851 the Virginia General Assembly created the new county of Upshur out of parts of three large mountain counties. At its county seat of Buckhannon, Berlin practiced law, bought and sold land, and earned money. In 1852 he had won election as commonwealth's attorney, what would be called state's, or district, attorney in other places.[19] When the census enumerator interviewed him on the last day of June in 1860, Berlin reported that he was worth more than $15,000, quite a substantial sum, but most of it in unimproved land that he had purchased on speculation and hoped to sell for a profit.[20]

The decade after the Compromise of 1850 had been good to George Berlin, and he understood clearly the significance of the two statues of the two great Americans. He wrote about it after he arrived in Richmond. His trip to the convention had taken him by stage coach from Buckhannon to Clarksburg, where he caught a train in the middle of the night and rode it through the darkness and all the next day to Baltimore, where he got on another train the following day and rode down to Washington, D.C. There he spent two days with an old Upshur County friend, Richard L. Brown, who had recently moved to the city. They saw the sights, visited the Capitol, and even attended the theater. The next day Berlin took a steamboat down the Potomac River to the rail terminal and another train that finally carried him into Richmond. One of the things that he noted with pleasure was that his boat passed right by Mount Vernon, where George Washington had lived and died, and his train passed near the site in Hanover County where Henry Clay had been born.[21]

Neither George Berlin nor most of his contemporary Americans could imagine that their nation, founded and saved by such men, could break apart. He still had hope for compromise. The members of Congress he had briefly met and heard speak in Washington had impressed him as serious and competent,[22] and even though they may not have been men of Clay's stature and talent, they were trying to find a solution to the national problem. But just as Berlin missed some of the implications of what John Tyler was saying, he had also missed the portentous significance of one thing that he had observed in Washington. Berlin told his wife that the leading Southern Democrats he had met and listened to seemed to be "generally strong secessionists & hate the Northern people here like the devil. But it is because they will soon be all turned out of Office in this City." That was not the only or even the main reason that Democrats were angry on the eve of Lincoln's inauguration. Still, Berlin placed his faith in the old Whigs, like himself, and went on, "The whigs are every where in favor of preserving the Union, and will succeed."[23] The members of the so-called peace conference about which John Tyler was still talking had been assembled there for the purpose of preserving the Union. They had not succeeded, as Tyler was saying, but as Berlin was not hearing.

In spite of the reality of disunion, Berlin persisted in his incomprehending disbelief during John Tyler's long speech and thought about his wife and his children, not about his imperiled nation. Finishing that sentence—"we now believe that harmony will soon prevail again in our Country"—he turned to family matters and professional business. Not only did life beyond the political crisis go on, but everybody expected it to go on with little or no change to their personal lives.

As Tyler talked on and on, Berlin thought about his brother Frederick, who had accompanied him to Ohio and then to Virginia, where they had married sisters and afterward practiced law together in Buckhannon. Frederick Berlin had recently taken off for Wirt County, in northwestern

Virginia, where drilling for petroleum created a small eastern counterpart of a western gold rush. Entrepreneurs and speculators thought that they would strike it rich there. That is what Frederick Berlin hoped to do, but George Berlin cautioned him that a safer and surer chance of getting rich from the oil rush would be to speculate moderately and try to make his money as an agent for the serious speculators, who had need of legal advice and services and would have to pay whether their ventures succeeded or failed. Maybe George Berlin made a mental note then to walk over to the governor's mansion some day, as he did two weeks later, and ask Governor John Letcher to appoint his brother a notary public, strategically placing him to gain the best information about the speculators' plans and prospects and earn some fees at the same time.[24] The governor was a relative by marriage; he had married a different Susan Holt, a cousin of Susan Holt Berlin and Maria Holt Berlin.[25]

While John Tyler talked on and on through his dismal recital of how the Peace Conference had failed to bring peace, George Berlin wrote all this to his wife, hoping that if she saw his brother or spoke to her sister, she could get his advice to the brother speedily; but he wrote to his brother that day anyway, although none of the letters between the brothers for that time period survive. He wrote a third letter, too, probably that night after John Tyler had concluded his gloomy report and other delegates had also talked about their hopes or fears. That night Berlin wrote a letter to his ten-year-old son Emory Lee (called Lee) and his six-year-old daughter Mary.[26] While attending the convention Berlin also exchanged letters with his firstborn son, twelve-year-old Frederick Augustus (named for Berlin's two brothers and called Gus), but those letters do not survive.

The letter to Lee and Mary does, though, and it is charming in its slightly awkward admonitions about good behavior and the wonderful sights to be seen in the city of Richmond. Berlin had never been there before February 1861. His letters to his wife while en route to Richmond through Baltimore and Washington and immediately after his arrival have the wide-eyed quality of the small town resident seeing a populous city (three of them!) with large public buildings, long wide streets, and great throngs of people.[27] His letter to Lee and Mary is much the same, but it is also an attempt to instruct them about a larger and different world outside of their familiar Buckhannon or nearby Philippi, where they visited their mother's aging parents who had recently moved there from the farm in northern Augusta County.

This is the parentally conversational way that Berlin began his letter to his children: "I have concluded to write you a letter and tell you something about Richmond. Well I will tell you first about James River which runs along the south side of Richmond and is nearly as broad as from our house in Buchanan out to Thompsons beyond Ridgeways mill & at some places it is twice as broad." He probably expected their eyes to pop. The beautiful little Buckhannon River, which gave its name to their hometown—most people misspelled its name, and George and Susan Berlin were no exceptions—was indeed a feeble stream in comparison with the great James River. "Ships and steam boats come up the River to Richmond from Baltimore," he continued, "& from the deep sea from South America & the West India Islands, from New York, Boston and Philadelphia & other places." The children might have known something about those other places from having seen pictures in *Leslie's Illustrated Weekly* or in *Godey's Ladies Book,* which their mother sometimes read. He had recently sent her some new issues of both so that she could keep up with the latest news and styles as a young lady of her status should.[28]

Berlin wanted his children to know that the reality was greater than they could have imagined and that he was there to see the wonderful sights, himself. He told them about the wonders with language and comparisons that they could understand. "These ships & steam boats are larger than the houses in Buckhanan & some of them are full of people & some are full of Coffee, & sugar, and some are full of Cotton & Rice and Oranges & lemons, & cloth & Iron & other things." Those commodities and others passed through Richmond, enriching the lives of its businessmen and their families, providing work for their employees and enslaved laborers. "There is one mill here that is twelve stories high & as long & wide as it is high & by the side of it are two other mills nearly as large." Nothing in the children's experience could have equaled such magnificence, so he made comparisons with what they could compre-hend. "They make 2000 barrels of flour there each day," he told them, "that is four times as many barrels as there are men women & children in Buchanan."

Berlin started a new paragraph, giving Lee and Mary a chance to pause just long enough in this recitation of wonders for the comparisons to sink in. "There is a Tavern here six stories high & so large that it has nearly 500 rooms in it and there are some times a thousand people stay-ing there, that is twice as many as live in Buchanan." Berlin was staying in one of those, himself, the Powhatan House. He had finally learned after he reached Richmond how to pronounce the word—accent on the third syllable, he informed his wife[29]—the name of his hotel, the name of a Virginia county, and the name of the Indian tribe and its leader in 1607. Going on, Berlin wrote to this children: "There are thousands of houses here as large & larger than our Court House, and there are streets here longer than from Buchanan to Georg Carpers with large houses close together on both sides all the way & pavements on each side half as wide as our streets in Buchanan. And these side walks are full of people hurrying along some one way & some another some black & some white, some richly dressed & some almost ragged, and the streets are full of wagons & fine carriages & the carriages are full of fine Ladies & gentle-men & pretty little boys & girls." The wonders ran on breathlessly, or so he probably hoped.

Then came the lessons. Another new paragraph. "There are a great many pretty little boys & girls here," he wrote. "They nearly all go to school & are very smart. The bad and mischievous boys are some times taken up when they misbehave & locked up in a big cage & their parents have to pay to get them out." And worse, if bad boys grew up to be bad men, they got sent to the penitentiary, a huge and scary stone and brick building standing high on a hill west of the hill on which the Capitol and the Powhatan House stood. From an upper room of Berlin's hotel the prison might have been visible through the city forest of chimneys and steeples. Indeed, it may already have been a joke in Richmond, as it certainly was later, that the outstretched bronze arm of General Washington, himself, sitting high on his prancing steed beside the Capitol, pointed directly toward the penitentiary, as if warning the legislators inside the building, on which the general's eye was firmly fixed, that if they betrayed his trust, if they jeopardized the nation he had helped found, then they would know exactly where he thought they belonged. Another statue of Washington—Houdon's life-sized marble statue—stood inside the Capitol, too, just outside the chamber of the House of Delegates, sternly reminding all the state's public officers of their responsibilities to the nation.

The "bad people" from every part of Virginia, Berlin continued, were "locked up in dark cells" in that prison. Some of them had to work "in close rooms & yards with high walls around them & they are not allowed to go out or to speak to any one." A few of the less wicked prisoners did maintenance in the streets or grounds keeping in the park (called Capitol Square) that surrounded the Capitol with its statues of Washington and Clay; but "they dare not talk to any person and there is a man standing by them all the time with a gun to shoot them if they try to run off." Even if prisoners ran off, they wore such conspicuous prison garb that they could not get away unnoticed. Berlin described the prisoners' uniforms for his children to let them know how ashamed they would be if their misbehavior should some day require them to be thus costumed and locked up with the wicked people of the world. He told Lee and Mary that "one side or half of their cloths is white & the other side is black & one side of their heads is shaved, & they eat corse food & all this they suffer for stealing & false swearing and hurting people & for other crimes."

For two more paragraphs Berlin described the sights and sounds of the city and told his children how much he loved and missed them and how speedily he would return to them just as soon as he could. He finally concluded, signed the letter, "Your Affectionate Pa," and went to bed; but the next day, before he mailed the letter to Lee and Mary, he returned to his moralizing and added a postscript: "just think how odd & laughable it would look to see a lot of people together with one side of all their cloths black & the other side white, and how badly they must feel to be dressed in such a manner & have every body that passes along looking & laughing at them & having a man with a gun watching them all day and then to think that when they have worked hard all day long are locked up in dark cells all night & get nothing but corse food to eat. This is the way that bad people are punished. How much better it is to do right & to be honest."

Berlin had no doubt that bad men were responsible for the political crisis that threatened the nation and drew him away from his family and all the way to Richmond. The current crisis had been long arising, but it had broken as a consequence of the presidential election in November 1860, in which four candidates ran for president, posing difficult choices for the nation, even more difficult choices for residents of the border slave states, and particularly difficult problems for former Whigs in those border slave states, for former Whigs like George Berlin.[30]

In 1852, the last of the presidential elections between Whigs and Democrats and the first election in the new county of Upshur, Berlin had voted for Winfield Scott, a native Virginian and a Whig. The original list of who voted for whom is in the state's archives and lists George Berlin among the Upshur County voters who voted for Winfield Scott;[31] but the Democratic candidate, Franklin Pierce, carried Upshur County by a margin of 439 to 324.[32] After that election the Whig Party began to break up, enabling the Democrats in Upshur County to win every election for the remainder of the decade by large margins. A good many western Virginia Whigs, including some of Berlin's neighbors, drifted into or voted for the American, or Know-Nothing, Party, which elsewhere in the country was appealing to anti-immigrant and anti-Catholic sentiment but in Virginia was attracting Whigs who could not bring themselves to join the Democrats. The Know-Nothing candidate received nearly three of every eight votes that were counted in Upshur County in the 1855 congressional election, not far short of the Whigs' showing in 1852, suggesting that the Know-Nothings were fairly successful in their appeal to the Whigs that year. In 1857 the Know-Nothing candidate for Congress lost Upshur County by a margin of 461 to 300.[33]

By the 1859 gubernatorial election, which Berlin's Democratic kinsman John Letcher won, the Democrats again received a large majority in the county. With no regular Whig Party nominee in the race, Letcher faced a statewide coalition of former Whigs, Democrats who questioned his fidelity to slavery, and perhaps some leftover true believers among the Know-Nothings. They characterized themselves merely as the Opposition.[34] It is not known whether in that election Berlin voted for Letcher, his family relation, or for the Opposition, his logical choice.

Nor is it known for certain how he voted in the intervening 1856 presidential election, which presented voters with three candidates. The county's list of voters does not survive, but it is extremely unlikely that Berlin voted for James Buchanan, an old Andrew Jackson kind of Democrat. He probably voted for Millard Fillmore, a former president and an old Whig and therefore a good choice, but Fillmore was suspected in many Southern states of holding intolerable antislavery beliefs, and that might have made Berlin hesitate to vote for him. Berlin certainly did not vote for John C. Frémont, the first presidential candidate of the new Republican Party and a favorite of antislavery leaders in several Northern states. The Democrats carried Upshur County by the comfortable margin of 533 for Buchanan, 296 for Fillmore, 10 for Frémont. Democratic Party leaders in the county were so displeased that 10 of their fellow citizens, all in the French Creek community south of Buckhannon, voted for Frémont that they published their names in the Clarksburg and Weston newspapers to expose them to public censure.[35]

The 1860 presidential election, in which four candidates from three parties sought the office, posed even more difficult choices for the nation, for residents of the border slave states, and for former Whigs like George Berlin. Again, as in 1820 and 1850, the spread of slavery into the western territories threatened national unity. Berlin definitely did not vote for Abraham Lincoln, who, although also a former Whig, was the Republican nominee and widely and accurately perceived as antislavery. Not one man in Upshur County voted for Lincoln. It is almost certain that Berlin did not vote for Vice President John C. Breckinridge, the favored candidate of most Southern Democrats and those who opposed all restrictions on the movement of slave holders and their slave property into the West. Breckinridge received 598 votes in Upshur County, nearly 100 more than Buchanan had received in 1856 or Pierce had received in 1852. Most of the loyal Democrats of Upshur County supported the Southern Democrat. Indeed, Breckinridge won majorities in nearly all of the western Virginia counties.

The other Democrat in the race, the nominee of its Northern wing, Stephen A. Douglas, received a meager 54 votes in Upshur County, suggesting that few of the former Whigs and those who voted for the Opposition in 1859 were willing even yet to embrace a Democrat, either a Northern one or a Southern one. Berlin was unwilling, too. He had always been out of step with the Democratic majority in Upshur County. His friend Richard L. Brown (who showed him around Washington in February 1861 and was one of the Democratic leaders who had published the names of the Frémont voters in 1856), lamented as late as October 1860 that Berlin still resisted becoming a Democrat.[36] It is extremely unlikely that Berlin voted for Douglas, especially when a good former Whig running on an ambiguous but unequivocal platform in opposition to secession was the fourth man in the race. John Bell, of Tennessee, would have been Berlin's natural choice. If the 10 French Creek Republicans voted at all, they also probably voted for Bell, who received 301 votes in Upshur County. Bell received most of the votes of the former Whigs and the men who in 1859 had voted for the Opposition. Bell lost Upshur County, but by a margin of less than two-tenths of one percent he won a plurality of Virginia's votes and received all 15 of its electoral votes. He also won the electoral votes of two other border slave states, Kentucky and Tennessee.[37]

The election of Abraham Lincoln led to the secession of seven lower South slave states. The Virginia General Assembly hastily enacted a law authorizing the election of delegates to a convention to consider what the state should do during the secession crisis. On Sunday, January 20, 1861, advocates of secession in Buckhannon nominated William C. Carper, a staunch county Democrat, but he withdrew, and a young lawyer, John S. Fisher, announced his availability about a week before the election.[38] Also on January 20, opponents of secession in Buckhannon selected Berlin to be their candidate, and the following day, when the county court met and men from the countryside were also in town, a larger meeting nominated him for the convention.[39]

Except when Berlin had been elected commonwealth's attorney back in 1852, he had never run for office and had not appeared to be politically ambitious. In this national crisis, though, he chose to try to help save his country. Berlin knew that the political situation was serious and that service in the convention was a serious matter, and he took his nomination seriously. He carefully composed an address to the voters so that when they assembled back in Buckhannon on election day, February 4, 1861, no one could doubt what he stood for. He preserved a handwritten copy of the address in his papers and docketed it as "My address to the people of Upshur Jan/61 when a candidate for the Convention."[40] It is in part a statement of principles, in part a lawyer's brief, and in large part an attempt at persuasion. It is unclear whether Berlin employed his "circular," as he called it, as a speech text or had it copied for distribution throughout the county.

It began, "Fellow Citizens We all admit that fanatical abolitionism at the north, has become so insolent and aggressive upon southern institutions as to be intolerable, we all admit that our rights & interests must be vindicated & maintained at all hazard, that the hand of northern aggression *must* be stayed"—he underlined the word *must*—"that slavery agitation *must* cease"—he underlined that *must*, too—"and peace & harmony restored upon a permanent basis. We only differ as to the mode, or policy by which these things shall be accomplished."

Berlin denounced secession and explained why he believed it to be futile or self-defeating. If the Southern states seceded, people in the South would lose their claim on the national treasury and access to the vast unsettled western territories. Worse, secession would not protect slavery. Hostility to slavery in the North was strong, but the Constitution and the laws, including the Fugitive Slave Act of 1850, part of the great compromise of that year, required Northern states to return people who had escaped from slavery to their Southern owners. But Southerners in states that seceded would have no legal way to claim ownership of refugees from slavery. The Northern, or free, states—including his own native Pennsylvania—would in effect constitute a new Canada on the very borders of the slave states, where escapees could run and hide, where antislavery activists could prevent their return, where they could actually foment antislavery activity in the upper South states, "rendering slaves so insecure in the border states," Berlin concluded, "as to cause them to be withdrawn to the south & put slavery in process of extinction in the border states."

Even worse, secession threatened civil war. Southern slave states might be no match for the more numerous armies that the Northern states could field. If war came, "no one can tell when or where it will end. Therefore," Berlin warned, "be not deceived when fools and demagogues talk to you about peaceable Secession." Some local men and other men elsewhere, as he acknowledged in his speech, were arguing that if Virginia went out of the Union with the states farther south, the united slave states would be in a better bargaining position to win concessions from the Northern states, reuniting the country on the South's terms. Berlin completely disagreed. There could be no such thing as peaceable secession, he wrote and called it "a vain delusion. And when the attempt is made it will be found to be *Revolution* in its most terrible, bloody & calamitous form." In the copy of the address the word *Revolution* is underscored; no doubt had he delivered his address as a speech, he would have given that word an ominous inflection.

Berlin appealed to patriotism, urging impatient men to give the spirit of compromise a chance to work again as it had in 1820 and 1850. He reminded them that as recently as the November 1860 presidential election, only three months earlier, 1.7 million Northern voters had opposed Lincoln's election and the platform on which he had been elected. If those sympathetic Northern men could unite with the true friends of the Union in the South, another nation-saving compromise was possible, but secession would destroy that opportunity. Berlin believed and stated in almost as many words that Southern secessionists were nearly as dangerous to the peace and union of the country as were Northern fanatics, on whom he placed primary responsibility for creating the dangerous national crisis.

As Berlin informed the voters of Upshur County, Americans everywhere had benefited from membership in the same Union, and until the most recent crisis erupted nearly all of them had regarded disunion as the most serious threat to their shared liberty and prosperity.[41] Reaching for their emotions, he rhetorically asked: "Is Our glorious Union, our happy Country & noble institutions of so little value, is the debt of gratitude we owe our fathers & our duty to our children so light & trivial, is our glorious flag, decorated with the stars & stripes, that has lead our Country to battle & to victory over hostile fleets & armies for 80 years & that protected American citizens in every quarter of the globe so worthless as to be hastily and inconsiderately torn to pieces & dashed to earth. Believe it not. They are the sources from which all our greatness, our prosperity & our happiness have flown."

On election day, February 4, 1861, snow and cold rain fell on most of Virginia, but men voted in large numbers anyway. As Berlin proudly noted when he later docketed the address, "I was elected by 885 votes my opponant getting 293." Buckhannon resident Henry F. Westfall recorded in his diary that day that the vote was 676 to 294.[42] There are no surviving election returns or newspapers that report the count. It is likely that Berlin received a couple hundred votes from other parts of the county that Westfall did not yet know about when he made his diary entry that night.[43] Whatever the margin, it was still a significant victory for the Union and for George Berlin. The Democrats of the county by a large margin had elected a former Whig who opposed secession instead of an active Democrat who favored disunion.

At the same poll that elected him to the convention, the county's voters also voted on a proposal to require the convention, if it decided that Virginia should secede, to submit its decision to a ratification referendum before secession could become effective. Elsewhere in Virginia voters who opposed secession voted to require a ratification referendum, and voters who approved of secession voted against it.[44] That probably happened in Upshur County, too, but the result of the county's poll is lost. Berlin no doubt had ample reasons to believe, as he left for Richmond a few days later, that the overwhelming majority of his neighbors and constituents in Upshur County, including lifelong loyal Democrats as well as old Whigs, shared his devotion to the United States and opposition to secession.

And so George Berlin went to Richmond in February 1861, where he hoped to cooperate with other Virginians who opposed Southern fanatics so that the nation would not be further divided, so that Virginia would not be forced into conflict with Northern fanatics. He and the other former Whigs who opposed secession won a large majority of the convention's seats—at least two-thirds, perhaps as many as three-fourths—and hoped to enlist the other border slave slaves that remained in the United States in crafting a compromise that would reunite the country. A majority of Virginia's white, voting-age men shared that hope in February 1861. In only one region of the state, east of the Blue Ridge Mountains and south of the Rappahannock River, did the voters elect more secessionists than opponents of secession. That was the only part of the state where more than half the population lived in slavery, the only part of Virginia where Lincoln's election appeared to be an immediate threat to interests more important than preserving the Union.[45]

George Berlin was one of thousands of border state Whigs who hoped that the Virginia convention could reunite the country and preserve the institution of slavery—preserve slavery in the Southern state of Virginia and preserve Virginia as a slave state in the Union.[46] He maintained that hope until long after John Tyler completed delivering his speech of March 13 and 14, and it was printed in the state's newspapers.

Bad men, the term Berlin had used when trying to persuade his children to be good, had brought the country to this pass and had taken him to Richmond, bad men who recklessly promoted an antislavery agenda in the North and other bad men who intemperately overreacted in defense of slavery in the South. There is no evidence in the whole corpus of Berlin's surviving correspondence and record of his public addresses that he ever had any doubt that slavery was a beneficial institution for the white people in the Southern states, even though he owned no slaves himself, nor did his brother Frederick Berlin.[47] His father-in-law, Thomas Holt, owned one man, one woman, and one child, and some of the more prosperous farmers, attorneys, and businessmen in Upshur and the surrounding counties also owned one or two slaves.[48] Slave ownership in that part of Virginia was not so common as farther east, but slave ownership was more common there than in the counties farther west. Upshur County was in the western part of a border region in Virginia where the importance of slavery and the number of enslaved people, if viewed from the east, rapidly thinned out. Of about 7,300 people who lived in the county when the census was completed in the summer of 1860, only 212 were enslaved (and there were only 16 free persons of color, as they were denominated),[49] a very small proportion compared with most of the state's eastern counties, but enough that white men and women in the county were accustomed to seeing enslaved people from time to time.[50]

From what Berlin wrote about slavery before and during the secession crisis, it appears that he had conventional, unremarkable attitudes about slavery and enslaved people. As his own circumstance illustrates, whether a man owned slaves was no predictor of his reaction to the secession crisis, although for many Virginians, ownership of slaves was a clear manifestation of gentlemanly status. In his part of Virginia there were slave-owning secessionists, slave-owning opponents of secession, non-slave-owning secessionists, and non-slave-owning opponents of secession. Berlin was a non-slave-owning opponent of secession, and although early in 1861 he might have imagined himself becoming a slave owner, he could not then imagine becoming a secessionist.

Berlin was a non–slave owner who opposed secession in part because, like a good many of the other men he met in Richmond, he believed that secession and war were threats to the institution of slavery as well as threats to the country. If he did not own slaves, it was not because he was opposed to slavery but because he had not needed to own slaves or perhaps could not afford the high price to purchase slaves. He hired an enslaved man named Frank to help in his vegetable garden and do other chores. He and his wife called him Uncle Frank. In an 1856 letter Berlin had referred to a man named Frank Little, which may have been the man's real name.[51] Tax gatherers, who collected taxes on slaves, and census enumerators, who reported on how many enslaved people resided in the county, were not required to write down the names of slaves, and they did not often bother to do so. Indeed, few white Virginians condescended to record the surnames of enslaved people or even accord them the respect of acknowledging that they had surnames and therefore human family connections. From time to time the Berlin family hired young white women or enslaved women (paying their owners a year's hire) to cook for the family and assist with the household chores.[52] Berlin's brother had hired an enslaved woman to help with household work at least once, too.[53] To that extent, even though they were not slave owners, the Berlin family fully participated in and benefited from the economy and the social system based on slavery.[54]

Berlin's experience with Frank was satisfactory, but his wife's experiences with the hired girls were not, neither the hired enslaved women nor the hired white girls. While George Berlin was away in Richmond, Susan Berlin complained to him several times about the difficulties she had in engaging and keeping the services of a proper white girl to help with the household and the children. One of the first of her letters that he received contained a complaint on that subject and a request, "I wish you would try and buy a negro there if you can get one cheap they are cheaper now than they will be after a while." She repeated her request a few days later.[55]

Berlin replied to her first request by writing, "I certainly shall purchase a black woman as soon as I can possibly raise the necessary funds."[56] In response to her continuing complaints about servants, he wrote a short little essay on different sorts of women, those who would be ladies and those who would serve them. He concluded in this way: "fair woman never was intended to be a servant, but was designed to be a wife, a mother & a lady equal in dignity & power & influance with her husband & then she generally fills her sphere well, with honor & credit to herself & family, and many of these hired girls when they possess reasonable intelligence make good wives & mothers, but are a nuisance in every other position. What a pitty therefore that every girl has not a husband and every woman a slave. If I had made the world I think I should have fixed things in that way. But so it is & I will have to submit & make the best of a bad institution so be patient until I get home & then I will see what can be done."[57] He never did buy his wife a slave girl, but in his surviving letters he did not explain why.

The blasé way in which the Berlins discussed slavery and enslaved people was fairly typical of white men and women of this time, Northern ones as well as Southern ones. Their attitudes reflected the values of the society in which they lived, indicating their identification with the better, more prosperous part of white society. George Berlin was a lawyer, owner in 1860 of more than four thousand acres of land in Upshur County,[58] a rising young professional gentleman with the appropriate perspectives. In his letter to his wife, he mentioned three categories: women, girls, and slaves; and from the context there is no doubt that he understood that the first two were white and the third black.

Southerners who owned no slaves but lived near people who did were not therefore naturally opponents of slavery. The dependence of white society throughout the South on the work of enslaved people for its smooth functioning was so pervasive that white people could easily fall into perceiving enslaved people as persons under some circumstances and as laboring property under others.

George Berlin did, too. Back in the summer of 1849, he had traveled to Alabama to look at some land that his father-in-law owned. On the way, Berlin wrote back to tell his wife about his journey. He had ridden his horse southwest from Augusta County, where she was then staying with her parents, to Tennessee, where he got on a steamboat and traveled several hundred more miles down the Tennessee River. The steamboat ride was a remarkable experience, perhaps his first, and he wrote about it with enthusiasm and wonder. The steamboat was huge and luxurious. The passengers were numerous and varied. He noticed many interesting things. In the middle of his account of the ride, Berlin told his wife a story. "There were a good many passengers on board the boat from different parts of the United States," he wrote, "some of whom were quite interesting & of course I enjoyed myself very much. One was a slave or negro trader & had a number of slaves on board but as bad luck would have it on Tuesday, morning about 300 miles up the River from here one of his negro woman fell over board and got drowned he paid $510. for her the day before but he did not seem to care and no one else took more notice of the occurance than if a blind pig had fallen into the River they did not even stop to take her out of the River, it is true she would have been hard to find no other accident occurred."[59]

The unemotional passage is in startling contrast to the tenderness with which Berlin wrote about his children and to his wife. It contrasts sharply with an affecting story that he told his wife in the same letter, in the very same paragraph, about a young white man whose wife had deserted him and their three-year-old son. The man was on the steamboat with him and was taking the boy to faraway Texas to try to start his life over without his wife. George Berlin was a romantic man who loved his family and cared about his reputation and his country. He felt his emotions keenly, and the story of the white man and boy en route to Texas touched him deeply. But the institution of slavery and the routine humiliations and brutalities that it constantly exhibited dulled the moral senses of everybody, even people like George Berlin who did not own slaves, to such an extent—an extent that he and most other white people probably did not appreciate—that without apparent moral difficulty he (and they) could equate an accident of a blind pig and the death of an enslaved woman—a poor and unfortunate woman who had recently been torn or sold away from her own family and familiar place of residence, driven like one in a herd of cattle or swine onto a boat, to be transported against her will to an unknown place and who could foretell what horrors. George Berlin wrote about ladies and women and slaves as entirely distinct classes of beings.

It was not the moral questions that slavery raised that worried George and Susan Berlin. It was the future of their family and their country. One day when a delegate was making what Berlin disparagingly described as "a sort of secession speech," he began to daydream again, and he wrote to his wife again. "I concluded not to listen to him, but write to you which is more agreeable to my feelings."[60] The previous day, on March 24, Berlin had received a telegram from Philippi informing him that his wife's brother, Stephen M. Holt, had died. Holt had just returned from a trip to Richmond to try to sell some horses. Holt and Berlin had talked about the family and business affairs, and then Holt had gone home to Philippi, where he went to bed with a fever. He took too much opium, in hope of breaking the fever, and slowly died.[61] Berlin did not yet know that his wife had gone over to Philippi and been present, together with her father and mother and sister-in-law, when Stephen Holt died and was buried. "I am grieved to think how sad & melancholy you all are," George wrote to Susan, "& how gloomy are the prospects of his family. Oh! how I pitty those poor, helpless little children," two sons and two daughters, all younger than ten, for whose support Holt had left few resources.

Berlin regretted that he was in Richmond attending to a national crisis when he should have been at home attending to a family crisis. He had not been there to help his wife through her grief. He had not been there to help provide for the orphans. He had not been there to help his own children understand death. Family matters like that worried him. He drifted off in another daydream during a session of the convention four days later while advocates of secession were continuing to press their case against the opponents of secession, who persisted in their efforts to enlist the other border slave states in contriving a compromise acceptable to all factions in the country. That made Berlin angry. He wanted to go home and help his family, but his duty would not let him. If any Union men left, he explained to his wife, writing while other men spoke, "the secessionists would possibly succeed in their disunion schemes & involve the Country in ruin. and if I were to leave now and the Union cause were defeated in consequence of my absence the people who sent me here would never forgive me, and would never entrust me with another office or trust." Already, he had missed a session of the circuit court where he had a good many cases pending, so many, in fact, that he flattered himself that the court might have had to adjourn for the simple reason that he was not there.[62]

Berlin disliked not being there to help his wife at the time of Stephen Holt's death; and he disliked it that other family business was falling too heavily on her, too. Because he had to stay in Richmond much longer than he had expected, she had to ask him what to do about his financial affairs. He had not confided in her about his speculations in land, his investments, his accounts with local merchants, and the like, so when their neighbors or acquaintances applied to her for payment of money that they said he owed them, she did not know what to do. Sometimes she paid them, sometimes she tried to avoid making a decision, but she did not know what to do.[63] She was frustrated, and he was fearful that unscrupulous men would try to take advantage of her, try to cheat him in his absence, or cart off the bricks for his new house.[64]

Susan Berlin and the members of her extended family now relied on him more than ever. Just as George Berlin believed that he should have been there to help with Stephen Holt's children, he also needed to consult with one of Susan Berlin's younger sisters who wanted him to help her get a divorce. Hulda Holt Diddle, only twenty-one years old but already married for six years,[65] wanted a divorce. She had a five-year-old son (named George W., in fact[66]), and she may have had a daughter, age three or four, and a baby girl born early in 1860; but surviving private letters do not give details about her family and troubles, and the few references to her and her family in public documents are either silent, contradictory, or confusing. It is possible that tax collectors or census takers misunderstood or miswrote her married name; it is also possible that they overlooked the family in 1860, which was not uncommon, or that her husband was temporarily going by another name, John Dean Jr. If the man of that name whom the tax and census lists indicate was living in Upshur County in 1860 was really John Diddle Jr., Hulda's husband, then he may have been engaged in some deceit, the nature of which is not evident but may have been the proximate cause for her desire for a divorce.[67] She certainly wanted and probably needed Berlin's advice.

Maria Berlin, wife of George Berlin's brother Frederick and sister of Susan and Hulda, also lived in Buckhannon, and Susan's parents and two other sisters and one or two younger brothers lived close enough, also in Buckhannon or twenty miles away in Philippi, that they could meet with and console one another and help one another out. Susan, being older than all but Maria, may have helped more than she got helped, but Susan wanted and needed help. George was not there, Fred was still away at the oil fields, and Stephen was dead.

Berlin worried that his brother was acting too impulsively in the oil business. He was occasionally vexed, too, by what he learned about their father, now old and remarried, who together with Berlin's sister and other brother Augustus had started life all over again in 1854 out on the frontier in Iowa. Berlin's stepmother and her daughter continually applied to him for financial help, and although he did not begrudge his father anything, he did not trust his stepmother or her daughter at all. Rather than send them any more money, he had instead bought his old father a new suit of clothes and tried to help out in ways that his stepmother could not object to or exploit to her own advantage. The mixture of affection and anger that recollections of the recent history of his father evoked gave George Berlin intense emotional pain.[68]

Still and all, George Berlin regarded himself as a happy man, a happy family man. On the last day of March in 1861, he wrote a love letter. It was Sunday. It was his wedding anniversary. George wrote to Susan that evening after spending nearly all day writing letters on business affairs and filling pages in his "memorandum book," a document now lost. Even as he wrote about business and perhaps about the law or politics, he had been thinking all day "about this being the fifteenth anniversary of our marriage. 15 years ago this day we were married." Through difficult financial times when they were starting out, through the births of seven children, during their sorrow at the deaths of two of them (their first child, Alice,[69] and their third son, William Lloyd[70]), he remained romantically in love with her: "to me you are still as pretty, & sweet as you were years ago." "I know that you have had a toilsome & weary life of it often." "I have done the best I could, & if I have done wrong at any time it was an error of the head & not of the heart." "But let us forget the pains & suffering of the past, & only remember its bright spots & sunny scenes & hope for the best for the future. But what do you say to 15 years more of married life with your humble but devoted servant, friend & advisor?"[71]

Susan Berlin was not beautiful, but she was pretty, prettier still to her husband. Her hair was dark, and she wore it pulled back tight over her head, after the fashion of the times, exposing her ears, which she adorned with stylish pendants. Her lips were thin and her mouth small, but even as her face looks directly out at the viewer from the one surviving photograph of her (perhaps the one she had made and sent to her husband at the beginning of 1862[72]), she seems to be on the verge of smiling. Almost smiling. People did not often smile when they sat before a camera in those days. Besides, a woman who had been in childbirth seven times in little more than a dozen years and had buried two babies did not always smile. Life was not all love and fun. Life could be hard, but unlike many other young women of the age, she survived the repeated, frequent pregnancies. Some people had criticized her in the past, perhaps because she was sometimes suspicious, perhaps because she could be quick to judge, perhaps because she had married her sister's husband's brother.[73] She had bright eyes, though, very bright eyes under thin, light eyebrows, and she had a small, well-shaped nose and a soft round chin. When she had her photograph taken, Susan Berlin wore a necklace and a brooch and lace instead of a collar. But it was the bright eyes, not dark or somber, that suggest a lively spirit. It was probably the eyes that caused George Berlin to fall in love with Susan Holt in the first place. Bright eyes and membership in a close family that gave reassurance in difficult times. Difficult times like these, with George away in Richmond and Stephen dead in his grave.

Susan Berlin had daguerreotypes of herself and two of the children made that spring and sent them to her husband in Richmond, as if fearing that he would forget what they looked like.[74] Of course, there was no danger of his forgetting what his wife and children looked like, but he was pleased to have the likenesses with him, to remind him of what was really important. Susan wanted George to have a good photograph of himself made in Richmond and send it to her so that she could remind herself of what was really important to her, too.

Hulda Diddle had her daguerreotype made that spring also and sent it to George Berlin in Richmond. He showed it to some members of the convention, one of whom pretended to fall in love with her on the spot—she was very pretty—prompting Hulda to ask later, in a truly bizarre comment that Susan reported, whether it was a white man who looked on her picture amorously.[75] There is much about Hulda, forlorn then, forgotten now, that the letters do not tell, nor do other available documents.

There is one photograph of George Berlin, taken several years later in Harrisonburg, when he was probably in his forties. He is standing there in a well-tailored dark suit and waistcoat, gleaming white shirt, starched collar, and black cravat. He confidently grasped the lower end of his lapel with his left hand and rested his right hand on a chair back. George Berlin stood ramrod strait, neither lean nor stout, his dark, close-cropped hair by then receding high back on his wide forehead, his brow contracted seriously, and his eyes, piercing bright eyes, fixed on a spot to the viewer's left. Here am I, the photograph seems to say. Here am I, a successful and respectable attorney at law, a Virginia gentleman, a dignified and serious man of affairs. His face was certainly serious. He, too, had thin lips, closed tightly while the photographer opened and shut the lens. His mouth was wider than his wife's and set firmly against the world's vicissitudes, against bad men. By then, Berlin sported a set of short dark chin whiskers, almost de rigueur in the final third of the nineteenth century, but he cultivated them later, and while he was attending the convention in Richmond he was clean shaven,[76] his firm, broad chin enough to persuade any physiognomist that here was a man of resolution and character.

2 Speech

THE CONVENTION CONTINUED TO HOLD BERLIN IN RICH-
mond, day after frustrating day, long speech after long speech, with occasional faint hopes of peace or reconciliation always faltering in the face
of bad news. He and the other opponents of secession continued to believe that they could enlist statesmen in the other border slave states to
achieve what the Peace Conference and Congress had failed to achieve: a
mutually agreeable solution to the national crisis.

Some time, it is not quite clear when, Berlin began to work on a
speech on the big problems facing the convention. Perhaps the long day
of writing in the memorandum book on March 31 was part of that work.
Certainly it took more than one day for him to organize and write out his
thoughts (for some members it took more than one day just to deliver a
speech), but there is no indication of how long Berlin worked to compose his speech, nor for certain when he began. He may have begun soon
after arriving in Richmond, but he did not say.

The only passage in Berlin's draft that can be specifically dated is a
reference about halfway through to a remark that Delegate John Goode,
of Bedford County, made on February 26, 1861. Goode noted that in
the states that had already seceded there were thousands of native Virginians whom he described as "our brethren, our kindred; bone of our
bone, and flesh of our flesh." Goode believed that Virginia should secede
sooner rather than later in order to take the lead in the Southern cause,
the better to defend Southern interests and slavery.[1]

Berlin disagreed about secession but readily agreed that many Virginians shared more with other Southerners and slave owners than with Northerners, and into his speech draft he added a specific reference to Goode's remark: "And here allow me to express my approbation of the sentiment expressed by the gentleman from Bedford (Mr Goode) when he so eloquently observed that the people of the Seceded States had sat down with us at our board &c. &c. that they were flesh of our flesh & bone of our bone." Berlin and Goode probably referred to the emissaries from three Confederate states who spoke to the convention on February 18 and 19 to try to persuade the delegates to join the Confederacy in order to preserve Southern slavery.[2]

Other than that one comment, there is no indication when Berlin began to work on his speech or how long he worked. Careful preparation was always the hallmark of his work. It was one reason for his success as a lawyer.[3] Berlin began by making twelve pages of notes as he compiled his facts, organized his thoughts, and tried out his arguments. The first page of the notes begins like a lawyer's brief and with echoes of his January address, "We complain. . . ." The rough draft of the speech also exists.[4] It covers twenty pages of paper, sheets of different sizes and shapes. It is very rough in spots, thick with emendations, dark with cancellations, crowded with new passages squeezed into margins. It is dense with facts and figures, but there are still some blank spaces indicating that he intended to go out and look up data in the census or in the tax records in the library in the Capitol. He worked very hard on the speech, polishing, correcting, adding an occasional rhetorical flourish. The work must have taken many days and perhaps many nights.

Berlin talked about the issues with some of his old friends who were also attending the convention, some of whom made their own long speeches. Even though he had probably never before been to Richmond, much less served in the legislature or been deeply involved in state politics, he knew many of the important actors on the stage of the drama into which he had suddenly found himself pitched. His wife was related to the governor's wife, and he spent several pleasant evenings in the governor's mansion in Richmond relaxing after a tedious or frustrating day of convention business. There, he met and talked with some men who impressed him as highly intelligent and principled, such as lawyer and planter Williams Carter Wickham, who lived in Henrico County, right outside of Richmond; and old John Janney, the highly respected president of the convention, from Loudoun County, northwest of Washington. Berlin also met George Wythe Randolph, a grandson of Thomas Jefferson, a direct, personal link with the founding of the nation. That was something. It probably struck Berlin as peculiar that Randolph supported the secession of Virginia from the nation that his grandfather had helped create.

The principal delegates from the Shenandoah Valley were acquaintances, too, men Berlin had met while studying law in Staunton or in the early days of his professional practice, men who knew his father-in-law, Thomas Holt, who had lived in Augusta County for many years before following his daughters and their husbands to northwestern Virginia. Berlin knew men like Alexander Hugh Holmes Stuart, a former congressman and cabinet officer from Staunton, and Samuel McDowell Moore, another former congressman from Rockbridge County. They were both respected Whigs, the party of old Henry Clay, the old party of young George Berlin. He knew John Brown Baldwin, only a few years older than he, the son of a judge of the state's Supreme Court of Appeals and a member of the bar in Staunton, perhaps the most talented bar in the state.

Berlin also knew most or all of the leading members of the convention from northwestern Virginia because in his law practice he had met them in court. Men like John Jay Jackson, of Wood County, a general in the militia; and George William Summers, of Kanawha County, another former congressman, another reliable old Whig, and the acknowledged leader of the convention's Unionists; and John Snyder Carlile, from Clarksburg in Harrison County, who had lived in Beverly when George and Susan Berlin lived there, who had sat in Congress once, and who was the most outspokenly loyal Union man from any of the western counties. Carlile was equally vehement and long-winded in defense of the Union and of slavery. He defended slavery against all criticism, even though he, like Berlin, was no planter or slave monger. Carlile owned only a few slaves but was long and loud in his denunciations of secession, which he, also like Berlin, identified as the second-greatest threat, abolitionism only excepted, to the institution. Carlile aroused more hostility from the secessionists in Richmond than any other member of the convention.

Berlin knew those men and talked with those men and listened to their denunciations of secession. When he had most of his data assembled and had outlined his argument in his notes, he began to compose the formal address.

"Mr President," he wrote, and as he planned to begin, according to the proper parliamentary form he expected to use when he rose, sought recognition from the chair, and read the speech to the hundred or more delegates who would probably be in attendance in Mechanic's Institute or in the chamber of the House of Delegates in the Capitol—the convention moved back to the Capitol after April 4 when the legislature adjourned. "Mr President I rise for the purpose of submitting a few remarks in vindication of the policy I shall pursue in reference to the Great Issue before us."

Berlin planned to state first that the crowds of secessionists who daily made their presence known to the delegates were not going to intimidate him into deviating from what he regarded as the right line of conduct. It had annoyed him for weeks that advocates of secession on the convention floor and other supporters in the galleries and streets seemed to be trying to force the issue before all generous efforts at compromise were exhausted. Groups of women sometimes tried to prevent opponents of secession from entering the convention hall until they promised to change their minds. He had written as much to his wife several times and would write as much again, later. He was supposed to act in the name of his constituents who had overwhelmingly elected him to represent them in the convention, knowing, as they did when they voted for him on February 4, exactly what he believed and why. He was for preserving the Union and for preserving slavery within the Union. He was supposed to use his judgment for the benefit of his constituents and the whole commonwealth and the whole country, not to please a minority of delegates—opponents of secession held a very large majority

First page of George Berlin's draft speech prepared for but not delivered in the convention.

on the floor until the middle of April—or a rowdy crowd in the streets. It was a heavy responsibility, and the weighty events about which he was preparing to speak were greater than any he had ever shouldered before.

It was quite remarkable, when Berlin reflected on it, as he did when he wrote to his wife on April 10, "when I consider the difficulties & troubles which I have surmounted and the ends which I have accomplished, for 17 years ago I came to this state a poor & friendless youth & in the midst of strangers in a strange land without an encouraging smile or a helping hand (but yours)"—George Berlin, always the romantic—"in the face of the strongest opposition I have work my way up to the head of the bar in my County & into the highest office ever occupied by any citizen of my County." The honor was not worth having, though, if the cause were lost or if, as seemed then to be the case, he had to remain in Richmond and away from his family even longer. "If," he continued in frustration, "you would allow me to sware I would say damn the office I wish I was at home with my Dear Sue and my dear little children."[5]

Not only had the convention gone on much longer than he had ever expected, but he had already grown tired of residing in the city of Richmond, which had seemed such an exciting and beautiful place when he arrived. "For two weeks I have not been outside of the Powhatan Hotel," he wrote in that letter of April 10, "excepting to go to the Capital & back and the Capital where we now hold our Sessions is not more than one hundred steps from my room. Of this I inform you to shew you how very tired a person will get even of a city. You soon become as indifferent to fine houses, palaces, broad streets, rail roads, crowds, & all that as you do of hills, mountains, forests &c, and then you want to reenter the family circle & be in the society of those you love & who love you. For it is only those of whom we never tire, & it is in the family circle alone that we must look for true happiness, and therefore I pitty the miserable wretch who has no wife, true warm hearted & affectionate, or the woman who has no husband, good & kind, to sooth her sorrows & alleviate her sufferings & sadness."

"The citizens of that portion of West Augusta," Berlin wrote near the bottom of the second page of the draft for his speech—he employed a very ancient description of northwestern Virginia that predated the Revolution, just as he still used the antique spelling *shew* instead of *show*—those citizens "are still a brave & patriotic people who love their Country, their *whole* Country & its noble institutions, as they still look upon this Great Republic as being a world within itself." He expansively and somewhat grandiloquently praised the geography and climate of his homeland, the rich natural resources of the mountains, the industry and productivity of the people of northwestern Virginia, and, above all, their love for the United States and the Constitution, "which they regard as the great Charter of our liberty & which in their opinion still stands as a glorious monument, attesting the wisdom and noble self sacrificing & disinterested patriotism of the fathers of the Republic."

That was a good phrase, "the wisdom and noble self sacrificing & disinterested patriotism of the fathers of the Republic." Berlin planned to tell the delegates, as others had already told them and as still others were to tell them, about the lessons to be learned from the political history of the United States; about how the founding fathers had sacrificed their personal and local and regional interests for the greater good of the whole nation; about how statesmen in the same tradition had fashioned compromises in 1820 and 1850 to preserve the Union; about how, when South Carolina threatened national unity "in 1832 & 3" by attempting to nullify an act of Congress, the nation's people supported the president in affirming the rule of law and "the power & efficiency of our Constitutional government." Wise men then had avoided rushing "headlong & rashly into civil war and anarchy & all their horrors."

"Sir," Berlin began a paragraph on page five, "the people of my Country"—that is, of northwestern Virginia, another old Virginia usage; one's home region was one's country—"the people of my Country yet look with pride and admiration upon this mighty Republic & its institutions for the prosperity & happiness of its millions of free & intelligent people, & rejoice in its growing power and greatness."

"And Sir," began the next paragraph, "they view with unutterable scorn & contempt the miserable aggressive fanaticism at the North &

the cowardly retreating propensity & inclinations of the south, which both tend to the destruction of the Country."

"But," a few paragraphs farther on, "it is alledged that the Northern states are hostile to our interests that they are an incubus upon our prosperity and a disadvantage to us in our march to power & greatness." Berlin denied that proposition and stated what he believed must be the obvious conclusion to be derived from the facts. The whole country prospered as a consequence of being united, and each region prospered as part of the whole. Northern enterprise had produced railroads, oceanic steamships, and industrial might that had created flourishing markets for American produce, including the productions of the slave states. The Northern states, indeed, or so Berlin claimed, "aided us in extending the area of slavery & in ridding us of bad neighbors," by which he meant the purchase of Louisiana from the French in 1803 and the acquisition of a vast southwestern territory after the war with Mexico in the 1840s. "And how has all this been paid for, Sir, out of the common treasury, whose coffers were filled chiefly from import duties, and as the population and consumptions of the North have been for many years nearly double that of the South, does it require the skill of a philosopher to see that the North has paid nearly ⅔ of that revenue."

Keeping those benefits in mind, Berlin went on to argue that the many advantages of remaining united with the Northern states far outweighed the injuries about which some Southern politicians complained. "It is therefore that I feel towards the Union as I would towards an erring Brother, whose faults I would conceal from the public gaze, whose unkindness I would bury in my heart, & for the return of whose affections & justice I would implore upon my bended knee."

Virginia, in particular, Berlin wrote, had a special burden and responsibility during the crisis of 1861. Almost every delegate said something similar. Virginians had been leading founders of the nation and authors of its Constitution, and Virginians had intimate connections with neighboring states. From the 1850 census figures, which he probably found in the library in the Capitol (the 1860 figures had not yet been published), he calculated that 183,051 native Virginians resided in the states that had no slavery, another 169,873 native Virginians in other border states that had slavery, and 35,135 in the states that had seceded during the early months of the crisis. "Hence it is that Virginia occupies a position whose power, grandure & sublimity is truly wonderful. She cannot be partial, her sons & daughters are in every state & territory in the Union, her affections radiate to every point of the Compass & like a noble & devoted mother whose heart is full of parental love & affections, with uplifted hands & streaming eyes she calls to all parts of the Union to come to the sanctuary of her heart & receive her blessing permit this cup of bitterness to pass away & not forget the parental, the filial & the fraternal love that has hitherto bound them together." Berlin argued that secession was not morally or economically or politically necessary or wise.

On page eleven, finally, he began to enumerate and emphasize what he believed to be the most important considerations of the residents of his part of Virginia. "Sir, Western Virginia can not agree to secession & a dissolution of this Union so long as she can maintain her rights & dignity in it." He reiterated what he had told his neighbors in Upshur County, that the Constitution and the laws of the United States protected slavery and the rights of slave owners, even if some residents in the Northern states disapproved or their legislatures enacted what they called personal liberty laws to hamper Southerners who tried to reclaim men and women who escaped from slavery. If Virginia seceded, "we could not legally demand from a Northern confederacy the restoration of fugitive slaves any more than from France or England or any other foreign nation whose policy is opposed to slavery." That was the first reason why northwestern Virginians opposed secession.

"2dly Western Va. is opposed to secession because by so doing a hostile foreign anti slavery nation would be brought to her border, thus inviting our slaves to run away" and make reclaiming them impossible.

"3d. Northwestern Va. is opposed to secession because the defence of our extended frontier would require numerous & powerful fortifications, a large standing army, which would be expensive & burthensome to the Country, demoralizing in its tendancy and always dangerous to the liberties of the people," summarizing and paraphrasing arguments against a standing army that were made at the time of the adoption of the Constitution and the Bill of Rights, back when the writing *burthensome* was common and writing *burdensome* not.

"4thly. Because as I have already stated in effect, it is an abandonment of our rights in the Union in the army, navy, treasury including New Mexico & other public property including the public territory." Even the "odious & detestable Chicago platform"—the Republican Party platform of 1860, the campaign platform on which Abraham Lincoln had been elected president—did not threaten existing Southern rights, that is to say, the right of Southern white people to own slaves. Besides, "three fourths of the southern people do not own slaves & tens of thousands of them have neither the means nor the desire to acquire any," and they, too, would be excluded from the western territory if secession made them no longer United States citizens.

"Trans Alleghany Va is opposed to the dissolution of the Union if it can be honorably avoided, because she is unwilling to pay duty upon her Salt, Coal, Oil, Cattle & other productions which in consequence of their vast & inexhaustible quantities & number necessarily seek a market all over this Union, and while in the Union we have a right to carry these boundless subjects of wealth to any part of the Country duty free which would not be the case after disunion."

That was the fifth reason, but Berlin neglected to number that paragraph, so he began the sixth reason, and one of the most important, as "5th."

"5th. Trans Alleghany Va. is opposed to secession because not less than four hundred miles of her frontier on the North & west are, in the event of war, exposed to immediate attack from two of the most powerful free states in the Union"—Ohio and his own native state of Pennsylvania—"while at the same time we are cut off from the rest of the State by a chain of lofty mountains in our rear, without a rail road communication in the State across the Alleghany by which you could come to our aid or we to yours in time of danger."

The sense of physical isolation and cultural alienation that many Virginians in the west felt when they thought about Virginians east of the mountains was palpable and sometimes irritating. In some places, such as in the northern panhandle, where Wheeling was a flourishing manufacturing and commercial city, Virginians had much more in common with, and did most of their business with, residents of the free states of Ohio and Pennsylvania. Their families married across the wide rivers and invisible state lines, and their natural lines of communication and easy avenues of commerce flowed away from eastern Virginia, not toward it. Still, the residents there were Virginians, even if, like George Berlin, they had moved there from elsewhere or even if, again like George Berlin, they had been born in a Northern free state. Their sense of physical isolation bred political grievances against the residents and political leaders of the eastern region and touched on several extremely important and pertinent points of public policy.[6]

Berlin had just mentioned the lack of railroad connections across the mountains. The mountains were high and rugged, to be sure, and during the first decades of railroad construction in the United States—that is to say, during the three decades during which George Berlin grew to manhood, moved to Virginia, and became a husband, father, and attorney at law, during the three decades before he started making notes and writing his speech—engineers naturally avoided driving headlong into high mountains. They followed water courses, old roads, and other easy routes, bypassing some areas entirely. A map of railroads in Virginia in the spring of 1861 shows two lines running roughly parallel to the coast from the outskirts of Washington, D.C., to the North Carolina border, and one brand-new line from Lynchburg southwest to the Tennessee border. Three other lines ran westward from the coast as far as the so-called Great Valley of Virginia immediately west of the Blue Ridge Mountains. One terminated in Staunton, in Augusta County, another in Lynchburg, where a break in the Blue Ridge was the northern terminus of the new Virginia and Tennessee Railroad, and a third in Covington on the eastern slope of the Allegheny Mountains. Farther north, the Baltimore and Ohio Railroad traced up the Potomac River through

Maryland, past Harpers Ferry, and then across the northern counties of western Virginia to Wheeling on the Ohio River. A connecting line linked the Baltimore and Ohio with Parkersburg on the Ohio River. It passed through Clarksburg, where Berlin had boarded the train for his ride to Baltimore, Washington, and Richmond. No rail line yet extended into Buckhannon, even though in 1855 Frederick Berlin and a delegation of county leaders, including both Democrats and Whigs, had tried to raise money to construct a railroad into town.[7]

The location of the railroads was in large part a consequence of geography and engineering, but the location was also a constant reminder to the residents of western Virginia of how the public policy of the state had always seemed to favor the residents of eastern Virginia, even when the stated policy was to unite the eastern and western portions of the state. For more than forty years the Virginia General Assembly had been investing substantial sums of tax revenue and even more borrowed money in the stock of private corporations that planned to construct canals, turnpikes, bridges, and railroads for the public benefit; but almost every mile of track that the assembly chartered had been built in the eastern portion of the state. Westerners often obtained charters of incorporation to build or improve roads through the mountains and construct bridges and charge tolls for their use, but those roads were not so expensive or useful as the speedier railroads. The state's largest investment since the 1830s had been in railroad construction, and most of the railroad construction took place in the east.

The apparent discrimination was not a recent development. Even before the American Revolution was over, enterprising Virginians planned to create a system of commercial waterways in Virginia. The first great links were to be two canals, one employing the Potomac River and the other employing the James River, to provide inexpensive freight hauling between the tidewater and the back country, opening up the western parts of Virginia, Maryland, and Pennsylvania and also the Ohio Valley to the markets of the world. The cost of canal construction was high and the pace slow, and by the time barge traffic was routinely available via the Chesapeake and Potomac Canal as far west as Harpers Ferry, railroad construction overtook canal construction. The James River and Kanawha Canal, which was to link the James and Ohio Rivers by a series of canals and locks and a road over the crest of the Alleghany Mountains, never made it much past Lynchburg. Both expensive canal projects benefited residents of eastern Virginia, but neither was of any benefit whatever for residents of western Virginia. The main reason was that the eastern counties had always enjoyed a large advantage in the General Assembly, which had the exclusive power to issue charters of incorporation, decided which railroads were to be built and where, and voted to purchase stock in them with tax money raised from every county in the state or with bonds that taxpayers everywhere in the state would eventually have to pay off.

Free Virginians paid taxes on their land based on its value, with improvements such as houses, barns, and mills making land more valuable and subjecting it to a higher tax. They also paid taxes on some items of personal property, such as livestock, fancy riding carriages, and other movable valuables like gold watches, silver, and pianos. The tax on items of personal property was in some instances set at a flat rate and in others on the value of the items to be taxed. Owners of slaves paid taxes on their slave property, too—recorded in columns alongside the taxes on hogs and cattle and buggies—but the tax on slaves was not calculated on the value of the slaves as property. The Constitution of 1851 had, at the insistence of eastern members of the constitutional convention, placed a limit of $300 on the value of any one slave that could be taxed. That allowed planters, industrialists, and other people who owned a great many slaves (railroad and canal companies also owned a great many slaves) to pay taxes on a proportionally smaller amount of the total value of their personal property than people who owned few or no slaves and paid taxes on the full assessed value of all of their taxable personal property.

The tax advantage for owners of slaves was in turn a consequence of the way in which representation in the General Assembly was apportioned. Until 1830 every county, regardless of its population (its total population or its white population alone) elected two members to the

House of Delegates, and districts composed of contiguous counties sent one member each to the Senate of Virginia under a system devised in 1776 and revised from time to time as the population grew and spread west. Even as some eastern counties lost population during the early decades of the nineteenth century and most western counties gained, the same scheme of apportionment remained in place. Consequently, residents of the numerous, small eastern counties who owned the preponderance of the state's slaves had long enjoyed a disproportionately large membership in the General Assembly, which had the exclusive power to issue charters of incorporation, decided which railroads were to be built and where, and taxed Virginians and borrowed money that they would have to pay back to subsidize the construction of railroads.

The numerical majorities that the eastern counties enjoyed in the assembly resulted in tax money from everywhere being spent in ways that overwhelmingly benefited taxpayers in the east at the expense of taxpayers in the west. This growing inequity, amounting to an iniquity in many westerners' minds, had been the largest bone of contention at the two state conventions that had made revisions of the state's Revolutionary constitution. The first, held during the winter of 1829–30, and the second, in 1850–51, eventually led to moderate adjustments of the formulae for legislative apportionment. Under the Constitution of 1851, the increasingly populous western half of the state enjoyed a small majority in the House of Delegates, but in the Senate the eastern half still had an advantage. Many westerners remained aggrieved.

As the market prices for enslaved laborers rose rapidly during the 1850s to twice or thrice what they had been at the beginning of the decade, that grievance grew worse, and western convention delegates suddenly brought the subject up again, here, in the convention in the spring of 1861, and demanded that all personal property be taxed on the same basis, on its market value. Ad valorem taxation of slave property was a genuine grievance that western Virginians wanted redressed, but it was also a bargaining chip. If slave owners, who predominated in the east, wanted support in the secession crisis from citizens in the west, where slavery was much less common, then westerners insisted that the slave owners were going to have to pay for it with higher tax rates on their slave property.

These divisions between the east and west in Virginia were very like the divisions between the North and the South in the nation. The existence of the institution of slavery was the cause of both divisions, complicating all interrelated political, economic, and social questions. Until 1860, residents of the slave states had never had much fear that an antislavery presidential candidate could get elected and appear to threaten the institution of slavery and the inequalities that it produced and on which it thrived; but in 1861 the crisis in the United States between the northern and the southern regions revived the crisis in Virginia between the eastern and the western regions.[8]

George Berlin approved of taxing slaves at their full market value, not at the capped, reduced rate. When he completed writing out the whole paragraph for his "5th." reason, which was really the sixth, why the northwestern counties were opposed to secession—the one in which he very pointedly stated that there were no railroad connections between eastern and western Virginia by which either could provide defensive help to the other, and by which he really meant that the eastern half of the state could not provide defensive help to "Trans Alleghany Va."—he may have paused before continuing; but he continued anyway and struggled to write a new paragraph that stated his beliefs and proposed a solution. The resulting paragraph was awkwardly worded, as he tried to persuade and not offend.

"Now Sir," he planned to inform the president and other delegates, "I am coming to a point that may at first appear out of order & will doubtless be unpleasant to some gentlemen although not so intended. For it is right & proper that no man here should be deceived at this time. It is this, the very cause of this difference in the defences & improvements between Trans Alleghany Va & Eastern Va & certain defects & inequalities in our Organic law present so far as the people of Western Va are concerned the most insuperable barrier to a Secession policy that can be conceived." Berlin made five deletions and added five interlineations in that clumsy draft for the third sentence in the paragraph, indicating how careful he was trying to be and how much difficulty he was having.

"Our Slave property is the cause of this great National calamity," he continued. "The people of the North deny the right of property in Slaves. We assert that right of property, & say that it shall be acknoweldged and protected. Upon this we do not differ. In the peace Conference the great object of the South was to obtain a more complete recognition of this right of property, & its more ample, & perfect security. One of those provisions (& one which every Southern man most heartily approves) is that slaves shall *not* be taxed at a higher rate than land, or in other words, that *Slaves & land Shall* be taxed at the same rate. This every honest man admits to be right & proper." The parallel between taxation of slaves and land in the territories and in Virginia was very far from as exact as Berlin wrote; in fact, he misrepresented it badly. "This equality & uniformity of taxation upon lands & Slaves you nobly & justly concede to even the detested & abhored abolitionist of the North, whom you look upon as your enemy But you deny it to your own friends & fellow citizens of Western Virginia."

Sharp words but not very elegant or persuasive phrasing as he tried to work his way through and around the complications. Berlin went on, though, through several more paragraphs that he knew would leave a sour taste in the mouths of the people who were arguing most fervently for secession. He used some strong language: "And sir this odious discrimination in favor of slave holders makes the slave holder odious to the *masses* all over the state, and is producing a very unkind & dangerous state of feeling against the slave holder every where." He included some more figures from the tax records and hammered home his point: "Now Sir in all candor I assert without fear of successful contradiction that amongst the masses of Western Va. these facts have produced a state of feeling in that portion of the state that if any delegates in this Convention from Western Va. were to vote for or favor an ordinance of secession before this injustice is removed, $^{19}/_{20}$ of them would upon their return encounter a storm of indignation before which they might well tremble." He wanted the eastern delegates to understand that this was very important and had potentially very serious consequences. If "disunion were forced upon them," Berlin planned to warn the eastern delegates, "the top of the blue ridge would be your border."

Frightened, as he expected his fellow delegates would be, too, at the prospect of Virginia also dividing as a consequence of the nation dividing, Berlin changed the subject without any transition at all. Had he learned something about theatrics in Washington or about debating technique in court or in the convention, he might have intended to pause with his dire warning hanging in the air before he continued.

Berlin had to caution the extremists about unanticipated ill consequences of secession. He had done that. He also thought that he had to explain his theoretical and constitutional opposition to secession, and he plunged into a new paragraph.

How might citizens withdraw their allegiance from a government? He could discover only one way, *revolution,* which he had underlined in his election address and which he had predicted could come only in a "terrible, bloody & calamitous form." How could a state withdraw from the Union? The Constitution made no provision for such an event. Secession was certainly extraconstitutional, perhaps unconstitutional. How could secession be justified or remain peaceful? Congress could admit new states but had no constitutional authority to permit states to leave the Union. Berlin also toyed with an unrealistic possibility. He suggested that because three-fourths of the states in existence at the time of the ratification of the Constitution were necessary to put the Constitution into effect, to join them all together, perhaps it might require three-fourths of the states in existence in 1861 to allow any one state to leave the Union. Just as soon as he stated the proposition, he dismissed it with ridicule. "The supposed right in a single state to secede from the Union at will is absurd," he wrote; "it reflects upon the wisdom of the founders of the Government and is at war with every object & principle of the Union as expressed in the preamble to the Constitution. Sir I can not believe that this government is such a miserable rope of sand & such a combination of folly & weakness, as to allow the right of secession at will."

Where would it end if allowed to begin? First one state, then another, then the whole Union would be gone. Berlin explained his beliefs with some more strong words: "Sir this doctrine was called treason when Aaron Burr endeavored to induce the western states to secede & join him in a southwestern Confederacy. It was treason in the days of the Hartford Convention, when the New England states determined to secede & form a separate treaty with England to get rid of the non intercourse & embargo acts. It was treason in 1832 when South Carolina passed an ordinance of secession"—a revealing slip of the pen, there; Berlin meant to write "ordinance of nullification"—"& was on the point of being forced back by General Jackson without a dissenting voice & seeing her dilemma she made a virtue of necessary & came back herself."

Setting up his conclusion, Berlin attempted to summarize the opinions of his constituents as he thought that he understood them: "Therefore we are opposed to secession & an abandonment of the Constitution & the Union & the rights & protections guaranteed to us therein, so long as our rights can be maintained in the Union, and that in our opinion slight & temporary delinquencies on the part of the general government in the enforcement of the Constitution & laws, are not to be hastily thrown into the balance in opposition to the great & glorious benefits & blessings that we enjoy under the constitution & those laws."

Berlin had just written, "so long as our rights can be maintained in the Union." He was a practicing lawyer, and he had to know all about contingencies and escape clauses and know that he had just set up a condition, the fulfillment of which invalidated all the rest of the proposition. Perhaps later, if Abraham Lincoln and the Congress, containing at that time many Republicans but not an overwhelming majority, became tyrannical, then the right of revolution remained. If the slaveholding states, Berlin wrote, "after having ineffectually exhausted all legal & honorable means to obtain a redress of our grievances, when the government shall have been subverted & we shall have no alternative left us but submission & degredation, we should resort to the last desperate remedy, the right of Revolution, not doubting that out of the ashes & the blood of that Revolution would arise peace & honor & liberty, for 8,000,000 of Southern freemen." But leaving 4,000,000 other Southern people in slavery.

Berlin, the Virginian and Southerner, the non-slaveholding proslavery Unionist lawyer, had just written what the secessionists were saying. The difference was that they believed that the conditions had already been fulfilled, and he believed that they had not been and would not be. "I am in favor of giving the northern people time & an opportunity to be heard," Berlin continued writing, "before we attempt to tear this hitherto great & glorious confederacy to pieces." In any event, he predicted that the Republican ascendancy within the national government would be brief. That party, he planned to say, had won election only because the Democratic Party was divided and the Republicans had seduced northwestern voters by promising something that they could not deliver, a transcontinental railroad. When the consequences of attempting to put the Republican platform into effect brought commercial ruin, "I do not doubt that the people of the North & west influenced by these considerations will rise up in their might & majesty at the first oppertunity constitutionally afforded them & will crush out Republicanism & consign it to the shades of oblivian."

Thus, the considered political thinking of George W. Berlin, of Upshur County, on the dilemma of northwestern Virginia in the days and weeks before the Virginia convention of which he was a member voted to secede from the United States. His draft speech, filling twenty pages, survives in his family's papers. One of his children docketed it: "Speech delivered in the Convention at Richmond, March 1861 by G. W. Berlin, who was a delegate from Buckhannon Upshur County, Va., afterwards West Va."

George W. Berlin did not deliver that speech. He never even completed the work of polishing it. Perhaps, because there are blank spaces yet to be filled in with facts and figures, he was not through gathering all his data and working out just what he wanted to say. Perhaps he was not yet satisfied with how he planned to explain his positions and warn his colleagues. Perhaps he intended to include some specific proposals to heal the sectional differences, as many other opponents of secession inserted into their speeches but had not yet formulated them. Perhaps other men said enough of the same things in their long speeches that he decided that yet another long speech was not likely to change anybody's mind. Perhaps he was afraid to speak his mind in this blunt fashion and fail to prevent secession, incurring responsibility in that failure for whatever disaster followed. Perhaps the rapidly increasing pace of events overtook him, and the war began before he could finish editing the draft, before he could make a legible fresh copy, before he could screw his courage to the sticking place and deliver the speech.

3 | Nightmares

On April 4, 1861, a delegate moved a resolution that Virginia secede from the United States. The motion lost by a lopsided two-to-one vote of 90 to 45, not 88 to 45 as appears in some reference works.[1] Berlin voted with the majority against secession, in favor of the Union. That was the most significant event that had taken place in the convention so far, one that made news nationwide—news in both nations, as the provisional government of the Confederate States of America was beginning to act like a real government, and the government of the United States of America was still not acting at all. Surprisingly, as much as Berlin had complained to his wife about the secessionists, and as often as he had repeated that Unionists like himself were still in the majority and that the country might yet be saved, and as much as he certainly understood the significance of the event, he did not mention the vote in any of his letters to his wife. He did not mention, either, that he had written, or was writing, a long speech that he hoped would help prevent disunion.

Three days after the vote against secession Berlin woke up early in the morning of April 7, from a frightening nightmare. "I dreamed that I had just gotten home," he wrote about it to his wife that evening, "& you & I were at a party, that we danced & had a very merry & pleasant time of it, but at last the party broke up and while I was getting my overcoat you started off with some other gentleman & left me alone I ran to the door & called you, rec'd no reply, but heard you all laughing & talking in the midnight darkness up the street on your way home. I went back, sat down & resolved never, never, to see you again, my sorrow & mortification knew no bounds, but my resolution was instantly fixed to fly & forever leave the Country. I would not submit to be disgraced & abandoned in that way I arose gathered up my hat & coat & started, but as I turned my face as I thought finally & forever from home I awoke & my heart was jumping as if I had just run a race, & I was perfectly overwhelmed with alarm for a moment until I discovered that it was all a dream. Oh how glad I was that it was only a dream, how rejoiced I was that it was not true."[2]

Berlin did not believe that dreams were prognostications of the future, nor did he attach any profound psychological meanings to dreams or extrapolate from the incidents of that dream to the frightening dilemma in which he and his country found themselves. He told his wife about the dream near the end of a letter in which he repeated again, following many other repetitions, how lonely he was in Richmond without her, how much he missed his children, how much he regretted letting himself be elected to the convention in the first place. "If God will forgive me for accepting Office from home, this time," he wrote at the beginning of the paragraph that concluded with the dream, "I promise never to do so again. What a fool a man can make of himself to leave his family & home & business for a little honor & flattery & praise from the world. What children & fools we are. Office, Glory & Flattery is all that some men live for and what a perfect matter of moon shine it is when you get it. I would not give one week the soft & tender carresses & grateful attentions & soothing presence of my dear Sue for the whole affair. But here I must tell you about my dream."

He told her about the dream to let her know how lonely he was, to convince her how much he loved her and hated being separated from her. He knew from her letters, now that the mail was again being safely delivered between Buckhannon and Clarksburg, that she was lonely, too, and perhaps he tried to shield her from the fears that plagued her, as well. Indeed, at the beginning of the letter, he confessed that he had been quite sick for several days and confined to his room, missing three sessions of the convention. "I was so bad as to loose six pounds in weight between Saturday & Thursday but it is all over now."

He went on to commiserate with her about her difficulties with domestic labor. This was the very letter in which he wished that every girl could have a husband and every woman a slave. He informed her about a few financial transactions that he would have attended to had he been at home and that if somebody asked about a certain large bill that he had already paid, she should not worry. He promised to return to Buckhannon soon and plant potatoes and other vegetables in the garden. He asked about the brick for the new house. He asked whether she had learned how the recent session of the circuit court had gone. "I suppose you were greatly bothered by the numerous enquires after me. I wish I could have been there." Had his brother Frederick returned home from the oil fields, "& if so what does he say & tell him to write to me?"

Within that budget of routine news and queries about home, Berlin told his wife the story of his nightmare. It was the only instance in the several dozen surviving letters that he wrote—and that she saved—between 1846 and 1862 in which he narrated a dream. During the earlier years of their marriage, while he was practicing law, Susan Berlin returned to her parents' house in Augusta County every year or two to await the birth of a child and to regain her strength in familiar surroundings and in the company of her sisters and with the affectionate and experienced help of her mother. While she was in Augusta County and he was at home alone, and once, during his 1849 trip to Alabama, he wrote to her about what he was doing, what their neighbors were doing, and about how much he missed her. It is inconceivable that he never dreamed about her at all during those eight periods of separation that in some instances lasted two or three months or longer, but in those letters he mentioned, and only in passing, but one dream about missing her and their first son.[3]

George Berlin was now entering his third month away from their home in Buckhannon, not yet an unusually long absence. He did not need to tell her the details of the frightening dream in order to emphasize how lonesome he was. He wrote about missing her in every single letter that he wrote from Richmond during the months of February, March, and April 1861. He wrote every week, sometimes twice. He repeated his expressions of love frequently, and he wrote movingly about how much he missed his children, too, and how much he wanted to be with them to help guide their emotional, moral, and educational development. But on April 7, 1861, he wrote about a dream that genuinely disturbed him, more perhaps than he stated, more perhaps than he may have realized.

It is easy to read George Berlin's frightening nightmare as a metaphor for the breakup of the Union. His dream was not about loneliness. It was about fear and rejection, about the breakup of affectionate, harmonious family ties. Berlin was not worried about the breakup of his family, but he was worried about the breakup of his country and of his state. After the happy occasion of his dream's dance, in which everyone participated and literally danced to the same tune, the company suddenly dispersed. As Berlin reached for the comfort of his overcoat before going out into the inhospitable cold, the other dancers left before him to return to their homes through the dark winter night. His own wife unexpectedly betrayed him, left him behind and went away with someone else, went away happily with another man. Putting on his coat and also his winter hat to protect himself in the cold winter night, Berlin was left alone and in despair, cut off from all felicity. For all that he sometimes joked to his wife that she might grow lonesome during his absence and try to catch the eye of some local man, for all that he playfully suggested that perhaps some handsome fellow at home might kiss her on his behalf, for all of that, George Berlin did not worry about Susan Berlin leaving him at the dance. His dream was not about loneliness. It was about the fear of rejection. It was about the breakup of the Union.

The breakup of affectionate, harmonious family ties, the story line of the dream, was also one of the metaphors, often the most moving metaphor, of the speeches to which Berlin listened (when he was not daydreaming) in the convention in Richmond. Opponents of secession spoke about the nation as a big family, its members sharing a long and meaningful history, prospering together, growing older together, sharing hard times together, having their internal disputes but letting their shared interests override their differences, each member, each state, each region the better for its association with each and all of the others. They talked as if secessionists were breaking up the national family, rejecting old ties of affection and mutual self-interest, rejecting their birthright of liberty in the American Union. The metaphor of the family was a strong and prominent one in the long orations of the opponents of secession in Richmond and throughout the United States. Berlin used them several times in his own draft speech, beginning with, "I feel towards the Union as I would towards an erring Brother, whose faults I would conceal from the public gaze, whose unkindness I would bury in my heart, & for the return of whose affections & justice I would implore upon my bended knee."

Supporters of secession spoke a similar language, of broken faith on the part of the Northern part of the family. Some of the men who became secessionists had finally had more than they could take of the preachy opponents of slavery who denounced slave owners as immoral and un-Christian, who sometimes contrived to violate the law and their responsibilities to their fellow citizens by hiding escaped slaves rather than returning them to their owners in the South as the Constitution and the law required. If Northern opponents of slavery denied their Southern relatives the right to take slave property into the western territories and keep slaves there permanently in that land that they had jointly acquired and owned—Berlin had written about that in his draft speech, too—those Southerners felt themselves cheated out of part of the family patrimony. Increasingly, it seemed to them, their Northern relatives were ashamed of the Southern members of the family for embracing the sins of slavery. Secessionists spoke as if the election of Abraham Lincoln were a legitimate cause to break up the national family, as if Lincoln were the man who had gone off in the cold night with their wives.

Those men worried about what would happen next if they remained in the Union: perhaps an outright assault on slavery in the Southern states, where the institution was essential to economic life as well as deeply embedded in every social, cultural, and political facet of the society. Hadn't Lincoln said three years earlier that the nation could not endure half slave and half free, and that he did not expect it to remain thus divided? Were the implications not clear? Did he not mean that slavery would be ended? Did not his election to the presidency signal the beginning of the end for slavery?

The metaphor of the family breaking apart was a shared language during the winter of 1860–61, each side, as is often the case when a real marriage between a husband and a wife breaks up, firmly believing and announcing that it was the other's fault. Berlin's draft speech included numerous explicit familial references, too. There and in later essays that he began during the Civil War, he repeatedly used the words *harmony* and *harmonious* to describe the good old days or ideal future days when all the parts of the national family had resided together or could again reside together under the same national roof and to attempt to rekindle in his readers or auditors a sense of how much curative power a genuinely harmonious spirit might exercise in bringing the national family back together again in spite of its differences.

George Berlin's nightmare was about the dilemma in which he was stuck in Richmond, not about how much he missed his wife or worried about her fidelity. He admitted almost as much a few days later when he reminded her of their conversations about dreams. Unlike her husband, Susan Berlin believed that dreams had significances, contained truths. She had already told him that she knew, after the postal service had been restored between Buckhannon and Clarksburg, that he had been receiving her letters. "I dreamed it," she wrote, "and sure enough you did but you will not believe this. you think it is superstition in me but it is not."[4] He had not believed in dreams the same way that she did. Not quite. But for reasons that he did not state, George Berlin thought that he needed to explain the nightmare.

"But you say," he recalled one of their conversations, "'I thought George you did not believe in dreams'. That is true, but yet sometimes they will make us think of the scenes & pictures they present to our minds, and these scenes are so life like sometimes that they vex and annoy us, although we say again & again it is only a dream, thank God it is only a dream, but yet experiences teaches us that occasionally there is a very striking coincidence between facts & dreams, & therefore our suspicions get the advantage of our better Judgement & of reason & common sence." But rather than yield the whole point, George concluded that reason and common sense "must however always tryumph in the end. So goodby dreams you cant come it."[5]

He conveniently ignored his other comment to her about dreams. "Dreams," he had written earlier in the spring, "always go by contraries, and are therefore always reversed."[6] But even that feeble dismissal of his nightmare could be applied to the secession crisis. Northern rejection of Southern slaveholding was the reverse of Southern threats of secession.

In Richmond, George Berlin missed his family and feared for his country.

In Buckhannon, Susan Berlin missed her husband and was becoming genuinely fearful for their personal safety.

She wrote to him every time that she received a letter from him and sometimes when anticipating a letter. She wrote some long letters, even though she did not like writing. She was not as well educated and had not practiced and perfected her writing skills. Expressing herself clearly on paper was difficult for Susan Berlin, and she did not even have good pens or good ink. She repeatedly apologized for her lack of eloquence and clarity and about the quality of her pens and ink. "I dislike to write," she explained to her husband, "and I would not write to any person but you under any Circumstances whatever at this time."[7] Knowing that her husband sometimes showed her letters to other delegates and reported on family affairs to relatives at the governor's mansion, she asked that he keep her letters to himself. "I am done writing," she concluded in a letter at the beginning of March; "you must not let any person see this badly written letter. my pen is so bad you will have to excuse me for writing so badly to you. I am ashamed of it."[8]

Unpolished though her letters may have been, they were nothing to be ashamed of. Susan Berlin wrote better letters than she may have realized. There is a directness and emotional honesty in them that touched her husband and left no doubt of her love for him or of her fears for the future. Missing her husband, she wrote him long letters. Sometimes, after the children had gone to bed, she sat up late at night in a cold, fireless room, in the winter, writing to her husband. His love letter, written on the last day of March and received just a few days later, made her feel helpless in trying to explain her feelings for him as tenderly as he had his for her. "You say that you think I will think that you are going crazy because you write such a loveing letter," she replied haltingly. She tangled up her next sentence badly in trying to explain. The tangle was its own explanation: "I only wish I could write one as loveing and make it read sensably but I cannot express myself when I write a loveing letter but I love just as much when I do not write so, as when I write loveingly and I suppose more so."[9]

Susan Berlin was accustomed to being separated from her husband from time to time. His law practice frequently took him to courthouses one or two counties away for a few days, and his search for good investments sometimes took him on overnight trips out of town; they had been parted for longer periods eight times during their fifteen years of marriage, once when he went to Alabama and seven times when she went to stay with her mother for several months to lie in, as they called it then, and have a baby and recover from childbirth. But this time, the separation was different. He had left home for an indefinite, extended stay, and the political crisis added an extra element of unnerving uncertainty.

Susan Berlin also had to be in charge of everything. She knew all about household management, of course, and the difficulties of finding and retaining a good servant. "I wish you would try and buy a negro there," she wrote on February 27, in the first of her letters that he received after the restoration of the mail service. She had engaged a local white girl before he left for Richmond, but she did not approve of the girl. "She is about the dirtiest girl we ever had. I do wish I could get rid of her soon. good girls are not to be had and all the negros are hired out for this year I believe perhaps you could get a negro in Richmond

Cheap." Susan had given up on hiring white girls and wanted to own a slave whose behavior she could completely control. "I do wish I had a good negro I would not give one good negro for a dozen of white Girls. I have had the trial of a good many of them."[10]

By the middle of March even the hired white girl was no longer available. She had "stuck a fork in her finger and it commenced swelling up and she could not do anything," Susan reported to George, "and I sent her home. she did not like to go much she wanted to stay badly. I was glad of it because I did not like to tell her to go and she was so dirty I could not stand it much longer." Susan Berlin told her husband that she would try to borrow a "black woman" from one of their neighbors.[11]

Susan gave directions to Frank, the enslaved man George hired to help out, for getting in the firewood and plowing the fields, and she went ahead on her own and gave instructions for the purchase of manure and timothy seed for the hay field, even though she had some doubt about the price of the seed and was not sure whether George would have paid as much had he been there.[12] She decided to plant potatoes and start some tomato seedlings and peas, cabbage, lettuce, onions, and radishes, after it appeared that George would not return home in time to begin the kitchen garden himself. She got help in the garden from sixty-year-old Henry Westfall, the man who kept the diary and had recorded George's February election victory.[13] She asked her husband to bring their little three-year-old son, Charles, a toy wagon from Richmond, and she asked him to find some inexpensive packing twine so that she could begin hooking a carpet for the new house that he was going to build with the brick and lumber he had already brought and stored on the island.[14]

Susan could manage those affairs and take care of the children. Those were her tasks all along. But she was at a loss what to do when neighbors or strangers came to the house and told her that George owed them money. One local woman applied to her in the middle of March for money she claimed he owed her, and Susan was perplexed. "I did not know whether she told the truth about it or not. I did not know that you owed her," she wrote to her husband. "I thought she owed you but I let her have it in that way. I thought you could get the pay some time if she did not tell the truth."[15]

Such incidents made George Berlin angry. "I dont owe them one red cent," he told her about one of the men who asked her for money. "He would possibly have been intitled to 50 cents or a dollar more if he had done his work right but as it is I had already over paid him. They are worthless lazy trash!" He told her not to pay anybody any money at all, "excepting for things which you purchase. For you don't know how false wicked & lying the world is, & you don't know to whom I owe any thing, & if such trash call upon you again just tell them that you know nothing about my business"—which was by and large true—"& have no authority to transact business for me of that kind in my absence"—which he was now making legally true, too—"and this course will releave you from all annoyance from them."[16] George Berlin did not intend to allow his debtors or social inferiors to take advantage of his family.

Some of his relations annoyed her, too. In the middle of March she received "five sheets of foolscap" from Catherine Berlin Will, his sister out in Iowa, with complaints that George's stepmother and her in-laws were spending all the money that he had sent "in buying finery" for themselves. "You ought to see the letter," Susan wrote to George in exasperation, "and I do not think you would do much more for them if you knew how little thanks you get for being so kind to them. I do believe that they hate you because you are too good to them. they take you to be a fool to send them so much money. they just think it is a pleasure to you to give to them when they are so extravagant. you just indulge them in it and it does the old man no good at all I am very willing for you to help Father but I do hope you will not send the old woman and Mary Jane"—the daughter of George's stepmother—"anything again for they just curse you for it."[17]

To which George replied the next week, leaving no doubts about his own opinion of his stepmother and her daughter, his half-sister. He was sorry, he wrote, "to learn that that old virago, that horrible old wretch has derived any benefit from my kindness to Father. I never sent her or

Mary Jane one cent because I knew their feelings towards me & their heartlessness & extravagance & therefore to prevent them from getting any thing I got Father some Cloths instead of sending him money to get them with, last fall. The vilest fiends are not more unprincipled than that old woman & she has implanted the same spirit & disposition in her cub. I will send no more for them to spend."[18]

Fortunately for Susan Berlin, she did not have such emotionally trying relationships with her own side of the family, which included George's brother Frederick, the husband of her sister Maria, who also lived in Buckhannon but was still off at the oil wells. Susan's younger and unmarried sisters Elizabeth (Bet), Margaret (Maggie), and Lucretia (Lucy) sometimes stayed with her or with their parents, Thomas and Minerva Graham Holt, in nearby Philippi; and Hulda, her unhappy sister—who had offered to sell the two calves that she owned for $10 apiece to pay George part of the $25 or $30 that he estimated it would cost to get her a divorce[19]—all of twenty-one years old and disappointed already in marriage—she moved in with Susan later in the year and did the work that the domestic servants formerly did.[20] The Holt family was generally harmonious (to choose a word that George would have liked), and that was a source of emotional support for Susan during the spring of 1861.

Her family was supportive especially when her brother Stephen Holt died about the same time that George was writing that bitter letter about his own stepmother. After Stephen returned to Philippi from Richmond feeling sick and treating his fever with opium, Thomas Holt sent his enslaved man Mit (or Milt or Milton) to Buckhannon with alarming news that Stephen was sick and might be dying. Susan arranged for a friend to stay with the children, borrowed a buggy from a neighbor, and rode to Philippi in the dark. For a night and a day and another night Stephen sometimes seemed better, sometimes worse. The doctor thought that he was improving, but he was not.

"I never saw any person look so distressed as he did just before he died." That is how Susan described the deathbed scene to George. "I think he knew that he was going to die and leave Jane"—Stephen's wife, sister to George's convention colleague, Samuel Woods—"in the situation she was in. When he was dying he looked at her and never took his eyes off and they closed them so she said she never would forget that look so pitifull and distressing. I cannot forget it myself."[21]

Stephen Holt died on a Saturday evening and was buried on Monday about noon, and Susan Berlin went home to Buckhannon on Tuesday. "I was very uneasy about home and was sorry I went but now I am glad as I found them all well when I came home."[22] Her emotions and fears then surged to the surface and poured out onto the page she was writing. Continuing without any interruption, she wrote, "And I thought perhaps you could come home to die too and I was uneasy about you and thinking about you so much that I would have to write to you to come home as soon as possible. I am afraid you will get sick and die. you must come soon as possible. I would not have you die for all this world and everything in it because you would be worth more than that to me. O I would love to see you so much this evening."

Before she sealed up and posted the long letter, which filled several sheets of paper of different sizes and shapes, Susan turned a page upside-down, picked up her pen again, and wrote, as if crying out, "come home come home come home." The words are completely detached from the flow of the heartfelt sentence that concludes the previous page and

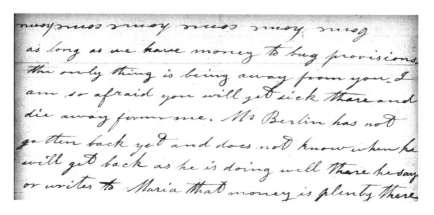

Page from Susan Berlin's letter to George Berlin, March 27, 1861, with her plaintive inscription "come home come home come home."

begins the next. Susan Berlin was lonely and afraid—"come home come home come home."

A couple of weeks later, the little two-year-old son of George's friend and fellow convention delegate Samuel Woods—Stephen Holt's brother-in-law's youngest child—died in Barbour County, near Philippi.[23] Woods had tried to get home from Richmond to comfort his wife during the child's illness, but he did not get back in time. It was "a sad affair to them," George later remarked to Susan, "as they think so much of their children."[24]

Just as George and Susan Berlin thought so much of their children, the five who lived with her that winter and spring in Buckhannon and the two who had died. Death was a constantly recurring fact of life. On April 12, George Berlin again awakened early in his Richmond hotel room. He had not been sleeping well, although this time he did not have a nightmare. Instead, there were noises down the hall. Men were loudly coming and going. A man was dying, died right then. "He hurt his foot early in March," George wrote to Susan that day, "& as he drank a great deal of liquor he got worse until it mortified & got all through his system & his blood became so corrupt as to cause his death, all the result of hard drinking. what a fool a man can make of himself, but it is so & will be during all time so long as men & liquor can get together."[25] George Berlin had once been a temperance advocate in western Virginia, and Susan Berlin would not have been surprised at the lesson he drew from the stranger's death; but she did not need to be reminded again of the many ways in which men might die, might die alone in a hotel room somewhere, far away from their families, from their wives and little children.

Heavy rain and flooding slowed the passage of the mails in the middle of April, and for more than two weeks none of George's letters reached Susan. When she finally received the letter about his illness and the nightmare, she began to have her own nightmares. She wrote him about them. She feared for his life and dreamed that he had been sick. Now she learned that he had, indeed, been sick. She dreamed about it, it was true, and she was frightened, not just that her husband might die in Richmond, but right there in Buckhannon, she was frightened, too. The secession crisis had reached such a stage that in the third week of April, when she next wrote a letter, families and friends were taking sides, and war and fighting were almost daily expected, even between families, even within families. Susan Berlin had frightening dreams at night and saw frightening scenes in the streets of Buckhannon in the daytime. Her emotions shot up and down, her desires conflicted with each other. She urgently wanted her husband to come home, and she wanted him to remain where he could be safe. The emotional strains pulled her to and fro, torturing her mind and also her words. Listen:

"I am afraid that some person will kill you before you ever get home we are all scared in town here I am afraid that they will come and kill us all here. if you knew how I suffer you certainly would come home, but of course if it is dangerous I do not wish you to do so, but keep out of danger for Gods sake. I wish they had killed old Lincoln before he ever got to Washington. he has no sense at all to make relations fight each other because they have a few negroes that he would like to have himself. I certainly have suffered death since you went away you never shall go away from me again to stay so long, if you ever get back. My dear come home or I shall die soon I wish you were at home I would not feel so miserable."[26]

Susan suddenly changed the subject there but did not begin a new paragraph. She seldom broke up her letters with new paragraphs. She abruptly changed the subject there, though, as if pausing briefly to calm herself before continuing, "the Children are all well at present." The fears then returned and took over again: "I have been dreaming about you so much, and bad dreams at that. I knew you were sick before you wrote to me. I told them so at the time I can tell a great deal from my dreams about you. you must be very cautious about yourself or you will be killed as certain as the world. O for God's sake come if you possably can get here I have heard so much about war that I am scared to Death allmost about you."

"Lincoln is to blame alltogether," she resumed a few lines down the page after another pause, "what business has he to come here and make this fuss and disturbance. we did nothing to him. he has no business to have anything to say about the negroes. he aught to let the negroes alone. they are not bothering him any nor I dont suppose they want to either. they would rather see him to the Devil than for him to act as he has and be free for ever. Oh George come as soon as possible and chase away dull care as you say."

Susan Berlin, who owned no slaves and only occasionally employed one to help in the house and who sometimes gave directions to Frank, wrote as if she understood the attitudes of the local enslaved black population. In that, she was probably just about as typical in her beliefs as George Berlin was in his attitudes about slaves and slavery, about as typical as most other Southern white men and women. Susan did not tell George that she had asked Frank or any other enslaved person for his or her opinion, nor did she say that she had overheard any enslaved people talking about the secession crisis. It is not very likely that she would have been present to hear such a conversation. There were not that many enslaved people in Buckhannon to begin with, and it is hard to imagine that a white woman with children to take care of, with a household to manage (and without a domestic servant), whose husband was absent in Richmond, and who had more than enough to do and to worry about, that such a white woman would have often been in the presence of enslaved people and would have paid much attention to their conversation if she had been. Perhaps she projected her own opinions onto other people. Perhaps, being a white woman in that society based on slavery, she could not imagine any other way in which any other person could interpret the rapidly changing and genuinely frightening events.

Susan Berlin signed the letter and put it aside. Later she picked it back up and wrote two more paragraphs as her fears accelerated. "I am so uneasy about you," she began; "indeed I feel like starting after you sometimes. Augustus"—thirteen-year-old Gus—"says he would go for you if he had the money to take him there. poor fellow he misses you so much. the little fellows talk often and want you to come home. they will not believe me when I tell them that you are comeing home. I tell them so often and you do not come that they do not believe me any more. I am afraid that you will not get home any more you will get killed, I am afraid before you get here. Oh my dear what would I do if you were to get killed and I never see you any more. Oh I would never see any more happiness as long as I live in the world again. I just might as well die at once. our poor little Children would suffer and die."

Terrible thoughts! Susan Berlin often wrote as she thought, ideas and incidents tripping over other ideas and other incidents, running on sometimes for pages without a formal transition or even a paragraph break. But she began a new paragraph here. We might imagine her stopping, taking a deep breath, composing herself yet again, and purging the fears before she resumed and tried to write some less-terrifying words. She began her new paragraph.

"The weather has been very warm here for the last few day's. there has been a great deal of rain. for several weeks here. the watters have been high but it is getting dry again." That was as far as she got before her fears erupted and poured out again. "I had a notion of telegraphing to you to come home that some of us were sick and you would be sure to come then but then I thought you could do some good there perhaps and I thought it would not be right to do so, but I tell them that you never will come back again when I think of it I can not eat or sleep either on account of your not comeing home I am so uneasy. do write to me if you are not coming home at all any more it is dreadfull times indeed now. If you ever get home any more I will tell you all the news. I must now close as it is late. I cannot think that you ever will get this letter's but I hope you will get it for I do not like to write you know very well. Write soon and tell me when you ever will get back. every person is wondering why you do not come back."

4 | Secession

GEORGE BERLIN WAS IN THE MIDDLE OF GREAT EXCITEment in Richmond. He still believed that the convention could find a means to save the Union, and that the convention would vote to amend the state constitution and finally tax slave property at its full market value, removing a divisive issue that threatened to disunite the eastern and western portions of the state at the very time when unity was absolutely essential. And until the last minute he still believed that opponents of secession would remain in control of the convention.

News that South Carolina forces had opened fire on Fort Sumter, a United States military installation in Charleston harbor, abruptly and permanently altered everything in Richmond. Berlin described to his wife the events of the day that brought news of the fort's surrender. "The South Carolinians have commenced canonading fort Sumpter to drive the United States troops out of it," he informed her, "so the war in that part of the South is actually begun & God knows when or where it will end. But we can suffer nothing from it if we can keep Virginia in the Union. But all day the secessionists have been wild & divilish with excitement and being informed this evening by telegraph that the fort had surrendered to the Carolinians they fired one hundred cannon here on the Capital square in honor of the event, while thousands of people were standing around cheering & bands of music playing. They marched to Governor Letchers & with music & secession flags & wild shouts called the Governor out & demanded a speech. He spoke but a few minutes & told them that he would stand by Virginia at all hazard. This they did not like & marching back to the Capital called out secession speakers who addressed them in a very excited & exciting manner & threatened to take Virginia out of the Union by Revolution if the Convention did not pass an ordinance of secession. They raised a secession flag on the Capital & swore that it should never be taken down, but after night Governor Letcher ordered the public Guard to take it down & they did so. You never saw or dreamed of such excitement before. You would have thought that there were no Union men in the City. Late in the evening I went over to Letcher's where I found many of the Union men of the Convention & after tea we (the Union members) had a meeting at the Capital & the Governor went over with us & we had quite a pleasant time of it. The secessionists haveing gone off in a torch light procession & kept the City in an uproar untill 11 Oclock at night."[1]

The city remained in a continuous uproar. The convention, too. Everybody was excited. Some of the most vocal advocates of secession had summoned and carefully planned what some of them called a spontaneous Southern rights convention. More than a few people believed that if the duly elected convention did not now vote for secession, the unofficial convention would take control of the government and take Virginia out of the Union by force. But that did not happen. Following the capitulation of Fort Sumter, Abraham Lincoln called for 75,000 state militia to put down the rebellion. There was going to be a civil war, and Virginia could not avoid being swept up in it because Lincoln called for 2,340 officers and men from Virginia, too.[2]

Some of the Unionists in the convention joined the secessionists as soon as they read Lincoln's proclamation. They had failed to prevent secession and to prevent war. Now they had no choice about whether to be involved in a civil war. Now their choice was not based on whether the slave states had a right to secede, whether secession was justified, whether seceding rather than remaining in the Union would better preserve slavery and the old South. Their choice was which side to take in the war. They could remain loyal to the United States but have to take part in a war against other Southerners, other slave owners, and even other Virginians; or they could join with their fellow Southerners and slave owners and fight against their own nation, against the United States, and against some other Virginians. For many of those men the choice was difficult, but it did not take them long to choose. When faced with the question of which side to take, almost forty of the Unionists in the convention joined the original secessionists.[3]

The delegates went into secret session to allow the members to express themselves freely, but some secessionists were through with free and deliberate but inconclusive debate. Former governor Henry A. Wise was one of them. He had joined in calling for the Southern rights convention that everybody expected to meet within a day or two. Shortly before the elected convention voted on the resolution for secession, he rose at his desk in the Capitol, pulled out a big horse pistol and a pocket watch, and harangued the delegates in a terrifying speech. Some delegates feared that he might actually shoot men who voted against secession.[4]

On April 17, 1861, two weeks after rejecting secession by a vote of 90 to 45, the convention voted 88 to 55 to submit an ordinance of secession to the voters in a May referendum. George Berlin voted against secession; for the second time in less than two weeks, he voted for the Union, for his country. That was what he had told his constituents back in Upshur County that he would do. That was his patriotic duty. That was his painful patriotic duty, even though he knew that the convention was going to vote for secession. The day before the fateful vote, he finally rose to his feet in the House of Delegates chamber in the Capitol in Richmond and sought recognition from the chair. George Berlin finally made a speech, not the speech that he had planned to make and on which he had worked long and hard, but a speech that distilled and drew on the long draft that lay on his writing desk back in the Powhatan House or perhaps rested on his desk in the convention chamber. The convention allowed each delegate ten minutes to explain his vote. This is how Berlin explained his.

"Mr. President," he began. "I would be remiss in my duty if I were to remain silent at this time. I am very reluctant, nevertheless, to waste the time of this Convention with any remarks on this subject, although

I deem it necessary to discuss it very briefly. I cannot submit, in view of the ruin that is to be drawn down upon us, and the policy that is to be inaugurated, to be forced into silence. Occupying the position that I do, representing a constituency peculiarly situated as they are, I cannot remain silent, and shall therefore avail myself of the ten minutes allowed me under the rule, to express what I feel on this subject, and define my position.

"What is our situation? We are situated beyond the mountains, isolated from the rest of the State by these almost impassable mountain barriers—cut off from all connection with our Eastern brethren or the South. The policy of this State always has been to withhold from us all railroad facilities with the Eastern portions of the State, and we are now left without the means of transporting troops or munitions of war to aid us in the coming struggle. While thus isolated from the rest of the State, we have an exposed border of 450 miles, stretching along the lines of two of the most powerful free States in the Union. In addition to this disadvantage, we are left without the means of defence. We are destitute of arms and munitions of war of every description. There are scarcely half a dozen guns west of the Alleghanies"—he meant artillery pieces—"while we are equally destitute of magazines. We are as perfectly in the power of our enemies, in the event of war, as any people under God's Heaven ever were; and, in view of this condition, you seem determined to precipitate us into war, which must inevitably result in our ruin, if some timely aid, not now visible, is not afforded us. But we may be attacked within the next twenty-four hours; and, situated as we are, on the borders of the powerful States of Ohio and Pennsylvania, we would be literally annihilated before you could provide us the necessary aid through the imperfect and difficult channels of communication by which relief could be sent.

"Would it not be wise, under these circumstances, to hesitate, and give sufficient time to supply us at least with the arms and munitions that are necessary to protect us from invasion? Situated as we are, if you take the action now which you evidently contemplate, you will render us powerless; you will force us to occupy a position of neutrality; you will place us in an attitude of revolution and resistance to the Commonwealth of Virginia herself.

"Now, this is the position that you will force us to occupy; and while we are forced to take this stand, from want of the necessary means of defence, you are fully prepared with all the means to carry on a war. You have railroad communications by which you can concentrate all your arms and munitions of war, and troops, at any given point, in a brief space of time. You possess these advantages over us, while you have the mountain barriers to protect you on the West, from any attack from that quarter. So that you may feel comparatively safe and contented.

"As it was remarked"—other western delegates had already spoken to this point—"the people of Western Virginia are the descendants of those who fought with your ancestors in times past. They are to-day a war-like people, and it is only necessary to say that they are mountaineers, to establish that fact, because no race of mountaineers have ever been conquered or enslaved when they have resisted.

"What is your condition now? You aim to precipitate the State at once into a war with nineteen free States, which can bring into the field legions thoroughly armed—not by a State Government, but by the General Government. Under these circumstances, if you force this war it must be at a great disadvantage and considerable odds. And then, when you reflect that you have a debt of $40,000,000 upon your shoulders"— actually $34,000,000, incurred largely to subsidize construction of railroads in the east—"you must necessarily see that if you precipitate this war, bankruptcy and repudiation must be the immediate consequence. You will destroy your property and your credit; you will block up every avenue of trade and commerce, and you will drive your very slaves from the Commonwealth. I would ask my Eastern friends whether we are now in a condition to resist an invading army of 75,000 men? I would ask them whether, in the face of an invading army of this magnitude, they would permit their slaves to remain here? I hardly think they would; and they must, then, necessarily see that the result of this conflict will be to drive this property from the Commonwealth.

"But I cannot discuss this question in a brief space of ten minutes. I can only say, in addition to what I have already stated, that I must, in behalf of my constituents, protest against this ordinance of secession."[5]

Two days after the vote Berlin explained to his wife what had happened and, as best he could, why. "Contrary to all expectations," he wrote, "the Convention has passed an ordinance of secession although a week ago there were two union men in the Convention to one secessionist. But the war policy of Lincoln has done the sad work. He called out seventy five thousand troops to force the seceded states back into the Union & to accomplish that end he required Virginia & the other border slave states to furnish part of these troops for the southern coersive war, And of course, Virginia will do no such thing as furnish men & means to cut the throats & butcher the southern people & as Lincolns policy forces to take one side or the other in this war she prefers fighting for the south, hence an ordinance of secession has been passed & if the north does not now desist from coersion we will very soon be ingaged in a terrible war & God only knows when, or where it will end. Our Country may be desolated, we have a dark prospect before us. Many members of the Convention were in tears during this week & often were so over come by emotions of sadness that they could not speak. We have been in secret session ever since Tuesday morning, and Richmond is beginning to look as if the war had already begun. Soldiers & officers & marching & to be seen every where. Companies have been sent to Norfolk & Harpers Ferry & three or four Northern ships have already been taken possession of here & at Norfolk, and a large quantity of arms & munitions of war. So we may really regard war as begun."[6]

Unionism almost disappeared from Richmond. Most of the city's and the convention's Unionists became secessionists. Some of the western Unionists with whom Berlin had been friendly left town as fast as they could to return home. John S. Carlile was the first to leave, the next day after watching an angry, menacing crowd assemble in the street outside his hotel. He sped back home to Clarksburg (Susan Berlin heard in Buckhannon that Carlile had been forced to sneak out of Richmond disguised in woman's dress[7]) and issued a call for a rump convention to meet in May in Wheeling, threatening to sunder the state of Virginia, as the secession of the Southern slave states had sundered the Union.

The unimaginable had come about. The nation had broken apart. Virginia might also break apart. Berlin had opposed secession, had voted against it twice, had spoken against hasty action before the final and fateful vote. Unlike the western delegates who left right after that vote, Berlin and a larger number of opponents of secession, including most of the western members, remained in Richmond, stood by Virginia in spite of its secession and continued to attend the convention. They took part as it created a provisional army for the defense of Virginia and watched Colonel Robert E. Lee come to town and receive a commission as a major general in that army. They also took the first steps to join Virginia with the Confederate States of America.

Lincoln's call for troops from Virginia had changed everything. Berlin's political and constitutional objections to secession were now irrelevant. The reasoning and arguments in his February public letter that won him election to the convention and also the enumerated objections to secession that he wrote into his draft speech were all suddenly beside the point. The decisions that Union men like Berlin made after April 15, 1861, were made on completely different bases than the decisions that men had made during the winter and first weeks of spring. Now, the decision was not based on policy options; it was based on the reality of war. They had to choose which side to take.

George Berlin, the Pennsylvania-born Virginian and Southerner, the non-slaveholding, proslavery Unionist from Upshur County, made his choice. The Virginia gentleman arose again in the convention on April 23. He had his old draft speech in hand or had its facts and figures in his head. "I rise for the purpose of making a personal explanation," he told the remaining delegates.

"It is known to all here that I voted against the Ordinance of Secession, and I did so at the time for reasons which were entirely satisfactory to myself, and prove a strong sense of duty to those whom I represent. My constituents, sir, were strong for Union when I last heard from them. I was elected as a Union delegate. My people were unanimous upon that subject"—exaggeration of a kind not atypical under such circumstances—"and I came here and thus far faithfully represented their views and wishes. They were devotedly attached to the Union for many reasons which it is not now necessary for me to state. I can say that I most heartily endorse and adopt what was so well said by the gentleman from Marion (Mr. HAYMOND)."

Alpheus F. Haymond, of Marion County, another western Virginia delegate, had just a few minutes earlier risen, as did a few other delegates who had voted against secession on April 17, and asked for leave to change his vote, stating in part, "my lot is cast with Virginia—I was born among the proud hills of North-western Virginia, and educated in your own Eastern Virginia, and I have no other feelings and am animated by no other impulses than those of a true Virginian; and so help me God, my destiny shall be that of Virginia, whether it be one of prosperity or poverty."[8]

Berlin continued, "My people, like his, were truly attached to the Union: not only because of the benefits which they derived from it; not only in consequence of the perilous situation which they occupy, and the relationship that exists between that region of country and the border free States; but from higher and nobler considerations than any of these. They were attached to it because of the power and *prestige* which that Union has given us among the nations of the earth.

"I will here state a fact which I know exercised considerable influence among my people. As early as 1856, there were 183,000 native Virginians in the border free State counties, and the ties of consanguinity which this fact shows to exist operated necessarily to produce a strong Union feeling among the people along the border counties in Virginia. But, sir, I have done my duty; and whilst I have been silent, my votes have shown, and now show, how I have stood. All our efforts for an adjustment of the difficulties that beset us, have proved fruitless, because of the course of the corrupt powers at Washington. All hopes of reconstructing the Union are now at an end. It is no longer reasonable even to conceive such an idea. Every hope of such a result is gone. This is not a time for Virginians to be divided; and lest my position and the position of the people of my section may be misunderstood; lest our position might exert a deleterious influence upon the people of the East, by being supposed to be that of hostility to this movement; and anxious to promote that unanimity so essential to the success of the cause in which Virginia is now engaged, while I have not heard a word from my constituents for a month, yet, assured that they will sustain me in view of the events that have transpired recently, I shall now ask leave of the Convention to change my vote on the ordinance of secession, from the negative to the affirmative.

"I have contemplated this change for days. I have been waiting only for one thing to be done, and that would have been done if gentlemen only understood the salutary influence it would exercise among the people of my section. I refer to the tax question. You all know that this has been a thorn in the side of our people. I will hazard the opinion that some gentlemen in that far distant border would be very well pleased if this Convention would take no action in this matter, but allow it to remain as it is, and thus afford these gentlemen an opportunity to create mischief." Berlin no doubt expected his audience to think about Carlile's incipient separatist movement.

"But in order to obviate such difficulties," he continued, "and defeat the infamous plans of that class of mischief makers, I had hoped that the Convention would see the importance of removing this source of difficulty, and doing that which would lead to conciliation and harmony among our people at this time. If they would pass this tax ordinance we could go home to our constituents and say we had done our duty, and having been defeated in our efforts at peace by the machinations of the powers at Washington, we changed our policy and went in for secession. Our Eastern brethren found it their duty to pursue this line of policy, and we aided them in it. But they have done you justice by adopting the *ad valorem* principle of taxation in reference to the negro property and we have no cause now for any misunderstanding. They would hail joyfully this change, and unite heartily with the East."[9]

Three days later, before the convention completed its business and finally voted to submit a constitutional amendment on the ad valorem tax proposal to the voters for ratification, Berlin left Richmond on the train en route home "by way of Alexandria, Winchester, Martinsburg & the Balt. & Ohio R. R." He had been sick again. It is tempting to suggest that his recurring poor health, like his nightmare, was another consequence of the emotional political drama in which he was engaged. In either case, he thought himself too weak to endure the ride over the mountains in the stagecoach from Staunton and planned to take the longer, easier route farther north. Berlin wrote to his wife that he was finally going home: "I will not get home before Monday evening. And I want you to tell some friend or other that if I got home then, of which I have no doubt whatever, I shall address the people (men women & children if they will turn out) at the Court House on Monday evening at 7 Oclock, as they will all want to hear the exciting & intensly interesting news & fact which I can then communicate to them." He asked her to get some of his friends "to put up a few notices of this intention of mine, if they think it necessary. They will all talk me to death if I have to explain to each one separately & of course they all want to know all that I can tell them."[10]

And so George Berlin went home from Richmond to his wife Susan Berlin and their five children in Buckhannon, having done exactly what he had told his neighbors before he left that he would not do.

George and Susan Berlin no doubt had a happy reunion. Because they were together again, they did not write to each other, and there are no letters to describe the scene or to record what he told her, what she told him.

George Berlin made his intended speech in the Upshur County Courthouse in Buckhannon on Monday, April 29, 1861. There are few surviving newspapers from that part of western Virginia, and none reported the event, but Henry Westfall wrote that night in his diary that "G. W. Berlin came home this evening from the Va. convention, delivered an address at night. Va. seceded and joined the southern Confederacy, caused quite a sensation."[11]

Berlin's notes for the speech survive.[12] As always, he prepared care-

First page of notes for George Berlin's speech. Upshur County Courthouse, where he delivered it on April 29, 1861. (Photograph courtesy of the Upshur County Historical Society)

fully in advance, although for this speech no text survives, only an outline. Still, we can listen in, as it were, and use our imaginations to fill
in the blanks with context and knowledge of the events of the winter
and spring of 1861—about the complaints that Southerners had lodged
against Northerners; about the failure of the Peace Conference that old
John Tyler had reported on at great length; about other attempts at
compromise, one under the auspices of yet another old Whig, John Jor-
dan Crittenden, of Kentucky; about a committee from the Virginia convention traveling to Washington to meet Abraham Lincoln to urge him
not to attempt to resupply Fort Sumter for fear that any move he made
would provoke war; about Lincoln's negotiations with Governor Francis
Pickens of South Carolina, and the failed attempt to resupply the fort,
the South Carolina bombardment, and the surrender of the fort; about
Lincoln's reinforcement of Fort Pickens on the coast of Florida; about
a mysterious sequence of fires in Texas in 1860 that some supporters of
slavery blamed on opponents of slavery; about recent violence on the
border between the slave state of Missouri and the territory of Kansas;
about the seizure of naval facilities in Norfolk and Portsmouth in Virginia; about the decision that the Virginia convention made to unite
with the Confederate States of America and send members to its Provisional Congress; and about the decision that George Berlin, like many
other Virginians, had to make about whether to fight with the Union
against other Southerners, or with other Southerners against the Union.
He docketed his outline, *"Notes of last speech made in Buchanan. May
Court H 61."* This is what George Berlin prepared to say:

I do not rise to dictate to you
We cannot all see alike
I will inform you of my position and my views when I was elected &
    their origins—
1 They carried away our slaves
2 They nullified the fugitive slave law
3 They abused killed & imprisoned our people
4 They slandered & vilified us in church & drove us out, in school &

poisoned the minds of our youth, upon the stump, in the Senate &c.

5 They said our Constitution was a league with hell & a covenant with death & must be broken up.

6 They said that there was an irrepressible conflict &c

7 They said the Country must be all free or all slave

8 They said the people would be satisfied when slavery was put in process of extinction

But this we could bear with while confined to their own Country & to a few

But it grew into power & aggression

They got up the John Brown raid

They got up Texas insendiaryism

They got up the Montgomery invasion of Missouri

They got up the Chicago platform excluding us from a common territory

They upon that elected a hostile antislavery Candidate to the presidency

The Southern people were alarmed & required guarantees for their security

The time had come for peace see my circular You endorsed it.

Here, he referred to his January election address, which he referred to at the time as "this circular." He went on:

The Critenden propositions were defeated & why?

The Peace Conference proposition was defeated & why?

The Virginia Convention Arkansas Mo. Ky & Tenn. took it up & were defeated & Why?

How was the Va. Convention treated while it held out the olive branch of peace?

The promise of peace

The evacuation of Ft. Sumpter promised

The fleet & army assembled at N.Y.
The Committee to Washington
The notification to Gov. Pickins
The assault upon Ft. Sumpter
They hue & cry of the adm. & the North
The object to give bread to the hungry
The falsehood of the allegation
The proportions of the armament proves it
The reinforcement of Ft. Pickins proves it
The trick to arrouse the people
The necessity of the Souths preventing the reinforcement as no
   guarantees for her security were given and without them she was
   determined to cut loose from the North.
The war cry was raised & 75000 troops were called out to coerce the
   South, to force her into the traces & we forced to take sides—
Although she had been thus wronged & insulted—
Although no Security for the future was offered to her
Although she was excluded from the territories & no indemnity
   offered
Although those personal liberty bills were yet in force
She must be coerced but not the North—
But still I voted against the ordinance of Secession because you
   desired it—& I was bound to vote to meet your wishes—
But it was passed & I was free upon that question
But when Harpers Ferry & Portsmouth were assailed, plundered, &
   property destroyed for fear it would fall into the hands of Va.
When our vessels were captured
When our ports were blockaded
When the Northern Government people & press were all arrayed
   against us
When the Northern friends whom I expected to rise up to vindicate
   our rights disappeared into the air
When all hope of relief was gone

When nothing but base submission was left
And when the North was rejoicing over our divisions I did change
   my vote for the sake of harmony
And now I am told that I sold my friends &c
I was asked what I got in the sale for my vote &c
I did not become your dog by your suffrages
I am a freeman & will act the part of one
You are free & I shall not try to influence you. vote as you please.
1 But why did the Convention attach us to the Southern
   confederacy—*aid & Tax*
2 But you sold us to South Carolina & tacked us on to her
3 The Palmetto flag—
4 Voting in Camp
5 Members of Congress appointed
6 Cant live under the Southern Constitution
7 But what is Northwestern Va. to do—*Why do nothing*
8th Only arm to repel John Brownites
9th The East & South dont need us.
10th And if we don't fight the North she certainly ought not to
   fight us
11th The South does not wish to molest the North & only wants
   peace
12th If the North sends armies here they will be met by the South &
   we by inviting Northern armies here make this the battle field.
13th We get up civil war here
14th Why should we remain quiet, in either event we must occupy
   the same position for If the North tryumphs we remain in the
   Union. If the South tryumphs we remain with Virginia
15th *I am for peace here*
16th *Conciliation & harmony*

Thus, the considered political thinking of George W. Berlin, of
Upshur County, after he cast his lot with the secessionists in April 1861.
Many years later his daughter Mary, who was seven years old when her

father delivered the speech, slipped a small note into the file of family papers: "I remember the speech Pa made in the Court House at Buckhannon when he returned from Richmond—The Court House was packed. I sat with Ma in a chair near the platform. There was great applause, but I did not understand what it was all about."[13]

From Upshur County's citizens who then agreed with him and had favored or had come to favor secession and who had gathered in the courthouse, Berlin's speech received applause; but the court room was not large, and at most a few score men, and perhaps some other women and children, could crowd in to hear and applaud the speech. Other residents of the county certainly did not applaud or approve. Berlin faced criticism and opposition as soon as he returned home from Richmond. "We cannot all see alike." He said that in the opening words of his speech. He endeavored to make them understand why he had changed his mind about secession when he did. "I voted against the ordinance of Secession because you desired it—& I was bound to vote to meet your wishes." But after the convention voted to secede, "I was free upon that question," and in the changed circumstances that then prevailed, he changed his vote. Following the surrender of Fort Sumter and Lincoln's call for troops, including men from Virginia, Berlin had decided that the federal government had broken its faith with its Virginia residents, had broken up the once-harmonious national family. *And now I am told that I sold my friends* &c." He had heard that as soon as he returned to Buckhannon. He was accused of selling out to the other side. "I was asked what I got in the sale for my vote &c."

George Berlin had made his decision and was already facing the painful consequences. The voters would soon have to make their own decisions and vote their convictions in the approaching referendum on secession. As free citizens, each man would have to make up his own mind, as Berlin had already done. He tried to tell them that, but if his speech followed his outline, he did not express himself persuasively. The events that followed his speech indicate that he failed to convince his critics, many of whom were his friends and former political allies, that having voted against secession in April 17, 1861, he had fulfilled his duty to them and was released from any responsibility to stand forever by that decision even if circumstances changed. Rather than rely on his stated reasons for changing his mind, he asserted his civic independence, his independence even of his constituents. "I did not become your dog by your suffrages. I am a freeman & will act the part of one."

That was not the language of effective persuasion. That was almost an insult. That was probably a mistake. Many of his former friends and colleagues and constituents in Upshur County denounced George Berlin for breaking his trust, as Berlin had denounced Lincoln for breaking his. In spite of Berlin's pleas for the unity of all Virginians in time of peril, in spite of his predictions that secession would allow the South to preserve its institutions and its liberties—the liberties of its white people— in spite of his prediction of Southern success in the armed struggle, in spite of his hope that however the conflict ended northwestern Virginia would come out all right, and in spite of his concluding appeals—"*I am for peace here . . . Conciliation & harmony*"—in spite of all that, he had not persuaded all of his old friends and neighbors who chose to remain loyal to the government of the United States.

George Berlin had crossed his Rubicon in Richmond, and now he had burned his bridge in Buckhannon.

5 | Separation

THAT WAS WHEN THE REAL NIGHTMARE BEGAN. There was going to be a civil war, and everyone had to take a side; and people had to take part, too, many more of them than had ever expected to participate in a war of any kind, much less a civil war that divided the states of the nation, that divided the counties and cities and communities within Virginia, that divided friends from one another, and that even divided families, too. The divisions were especially painful and dramatic in places like Buckhannon and Upshur County, divided border communities in the divided border states, where personal ties of family and friendship broke apart, as did old and affectionate relationships.[1]

Some of the first fighting took place in such divided communities in western Virginia, and some of the most bitter hatreds sprouted first in those divided communities. The Civil War was real there and uncivil in places like Buckhannon and Upshur County before it was a reality anywhere else. Throughout the mountain South, throughout the four years of the Civil War, those divided communities experienced violence and bitterness that differed from what other Southerners experienced, and their experiences left lasting and different legacies of recrimination and resentment.[2]

The nation was divided. The nation was going to war with itself. In Virginia's eastern counties and cities the May 23, 1861, referendum overwhelmingly endorsed the convention's decision to secede from the United States. In the western counties there was much opposition, and in the Ohio Valley counties voters rejected secession by large majorities. An incomplete set of surviving results from Upshur County show that a very large majority of voters opposed secession, a larger majority in favor of remaining in the Union late in May than the margin by which George Berlin had won election to the convention as an opponent of secession at the beginning of February. The speech that he made in the courthouse at the end of April had not carried his county along with him, as he had predicted before he left Richmond. George W. Berlin voted to ratify the ordinance of secession, but although his brother Frederick Berlin got back from the oil fields of Wirt County just in time, the incomplete surviving tally sheets do not recorded him as voting.[3] Perhaps he did not vote, but George did not persuade Frederick that the decision he had made in Richmond was right.

As in Upshur County, in most of the western counties and cities of Virginia, a majority of the voters rejected secession. People were taking sides, and it was not pleasant. Among Berlin's neighbors, Albert Reger took command of a company of men who approved of secession and prepared them to fight for the new Confederacy; his brother John W. Reger took command of a company of men who disapproved of secession and prepared them to fight for the old Union.[4] Sixty-year-old colonel Henry Westfall, who had helped Susan Berlin with George's garden in the spring and who spent an evening with George after his return from Richmond and worked in the garden with him on another day, drilled a company of soldiers to save the Union.[5]

The outline for Berlin's courthouse speech contained a sentence suggesting that if residents in that part of the state remained neutral and resolved to *"do nothing,"* neither army would have an occasion to come there; but in the draft speech that he had prepared in Richmond he predicted that armies from the free states of Ohio and Pennsylvania would easily seize control of northwestern Virginia. His hope that the people there could let the extremists fight it out elsewhere was unrealistic. His prediction about the vulnerability of northwestern Virginia and Susan Berlin's fears for their personal safety were both proved sound.

A few days after the referendum on secession, hastily raised volunteer armies and militiamen from eastern Virginia and from Indiana and Ohio marched from opposite directions into northwestern Virginia. They met early in the morning of June 3. Soldiers loyal to the United States surprised and routed soldiers loyal to the Confederate States at Philippi, where Susan's parents lived. The Virginia soldiers panicked and fled, earning the event in Northern annals the comical designation the Philippi Races. Amateurish though the two armies then still were, there was nothing comical about actual fighting. One man was killed. More men were going to die.

George Berlin had to flee for his life. On June 11, shortly before Northern soldiers entered Buckhannon, Berlin fled his own hometown, leaving home "so suddenly," he later wrote, "as to be unable to remove either my family or my personal estate."[6] He was in genuine danger. People in those communities were organizing to kill each other. Berlin rode east toward Richmond to attend another session of the convention that was acting in place of the legislature to raise an army, unite Virginia with the Confederacy, make Richmond the capital of the new nation, and thereby inadvertently make Virginia the bloody battleground where much of the war in the east was fought.

In spite of his protestations to his wife in all those letters written during his first stay in Richmond that he would never allow himself for whatever reason to be drawn away from his family again on mere public business, Berlin fled from Buckhannon to save his life, and he returned to Richmond to do what he believed was the duty that he shouldered when he made his fateful decision. He rode east through the mountains for four days, "getting along finely and safely but slowly," as far as Monterey in Highland County, where he paused and sent a brief note home to let his wife know that so far, at least, he was safe. He boasted that on his ride he "had the company and enjoyed the society of Generals, Colonels, Captains &c. &c." The officers seemed confident, and they talked with the honorable gentleman, the delegate from Upshur County, about their plans and prospects. Berlin was feeling in the know and important. "I could give you very cheering news if allowed to do so," he wrote Susan, "But no one is at liberty to give accounts of the movement of Confeder-

An Ordinance

to repeal the ratification of the Constitution of the United States of America, by the State of Virginia, and to resume all the rights and powers granted under said Constitution.

The people of Virginia, in their ratification of the Constitution of the United States of America, adopted by them in Convention, on the twenty fifth day of June, in the year of our Lord one thousand seven hundred and eighty eight, having declared that the powers granted under said Constitution were derived from the people of the United States, and might be resumed whensoever the same should be perverted to their injury and oppression, and the Federal Government having perverted said powers not only to the injury of the **people of Virginia**, but to the oppression of the Southern Slaveholding States;

Now, therefore, we, the people of Virginia, do declare and ordain, That the ordinance adopted by the people of this State in Convention, on the twenty fifth day of June, in the year of our Lord one thousand seven hundred and eighty eight, whereby the Constitution of the United States of America was ratified, and all acts of the General Assembly of this State ratifying or adopting amendments to said Constitution, are hereby **repealed and abrogated**; that the union between the State of Virginia and the other States under the Constitution aforesaid, is hereby dissolved, and that the State of Virginia is in the full possession and exercise of all the rights of sovereignty which belong and appertain to a **free and independent State**.

And they do further declare, That said Constitution of the United States of America is no longer binding on any of the citizens of this State.

This ordinance shall take effect and be an act of this day when ratified by a majority of the votes of the people of this State, cast at a poll to be taken thereon on the fourth Thursday in May next, in pursuance of a schedule hereafter to be enacted.

Done in Convention in the City of Richmond on the seventeenth day of April, in the year of our Lord one thousand eight hundred and sixty one, and in the eighty fifth year of the **Commonwealth of Virginia**.

ate (Southern) troops." Few people then believed that the contest would last very long.[7]

Berlin continued to worry. When he left home, Frederick Berlin was thinking of volunteering to help put down the rebellion. George asked Susan to continue the attempt at persuasion that he had begun. "I beg him for Gods sake & for his families & mine not to take such a part against Virginia as will subject him to the loss of his property or subject him to the penalties of treason but to occupy a position of nutrality if he can not do any thing else."[8] The Berlin family was divided, too, just as the Reger family was, just as many others were.

George Berlin sent another letter to Susan after reaching Richmond. He repeated and enlarged on his concern for his brother. "I hope & pray God most fervently," he wrote, "that Brother F. will be quiet & not take such a part against the state as will sacrifice his life, his property & every thing that is dear to us. I don't ask him to abandon his principles but his action cannot avert consequences nor change them one man in millions is like a drop in the sea why then can he not be quiet & not make war upon a state that has protected him for years, that gave him a wife true & affectionate, that is the native state of his children & that has by its laws afforded him such a wide field for speculation & pecuniary advancements. Tell Maria to use all her power & influance without reservation or fear as she values her welfare, his life & her families future happiness to keep Brother out of that awfully horrible & distructive vortex of that fearful revolution against Virginia now rising up in Northwestern Virginia."[9] The men had not been able to prevent the nation from dividing, but if the men could not keep the family from dividing, perhaps the women could.

Berlin reached Richmond by train from Staunton at mid-afternoon on June 16, in time to attend most of the short second session of the convention and to sign the ceremonial copy of the Ordinance of Seces-

Facing page: Ceremonial Ordinance of Secession, with detail showing George Berlin's signature, added after he returned to Richmond from Buckhannon on June 16, 1861. (Library of Virginia)

sion. He refused to vote, though, on June 28 and 29, when the convention expelled twelve members from western counties, his colleagues and companions during the spring debates.[10] They had remained publicly loyal to the United States and organized the first of a series of conventions in Wheeling that led, eventually, to the formation of the new state of West Virginia—seceding, as it were, from Virginia, after Virginia seceded from the United States. Virginia was divided, too.

The impending division of Virginia, about which Berlin had warned before leaving Richmond late in April, had finally forced the convention to act on the question of taxing slaves according to their market value, that grievance about which other westerners had been complaining for years and about which he had written at length and spoken briefly during the first session of the convention. The day after Berlin left Richmond, the convention, hoping to hold the state together while the nation was splitting apart, finally recommended an amendment to the state constitution to require that all property in the state be taxed on the basis of its market value; but even then, the eastern delegates, representing the owners of the largest number of the state's enslaved people, refused to give up all of their advantage and slipped in a clause allowing exemptions by a vote of a majority of all members elected to each house of the General Assembly. That clause could still give owners of slaves in the east a chance to argue their way out of equal ad valorem taxation.[11] Nearly all of the western voters together with a notably smaller proportion of eastern voters had ratified the amendment in May.[12]

Berlin planned to return home to Buckhannon as soon as the June session of the convention concluded its business, but he did not. He could not. There was no safe way for a secessionist to get through the mountains and military lines. He made it as far as Beverly, in Randolph County, the town where he and Susan had lived for about three years after they married.[13] He was there on July 11 and consulted with Confederate officers at the time of the Battle of Cheat Mountain, another defeat for the Virginians, for the Confederates.[14] Some of the other convention delegates were there, too, including John N. Hughes, the Randolph

County member, who somehow got caught between the lines and was killed in an exchange of rifle fire.

Susan Berlin remained in Buckhannon with the children. The news of Hughes's death, if it reached her, even if the identify of the delegate who was killed was accurately reported to her, no doubt amplified her anxiety. Soon after her husband left on June 11, the Northern army occupied Buckhannon.[15] Unionists accused and abused secessionists and later in the summer began arresting leading secessionists and imprisoning them at Camp Chase near Columbus, Ohio. When the army entered Buckhannon, the town's Unionists turned out to greet the army, and loyal women who supported the Union made a point of attending a parade on June 15, but secessionists made themselves inconspicuous.[16] Susan Berlin's understated comment on the events was that "our town is very lively at present but I think of the absent ones sometimes which makes me feel sad and lonely."[17]

Susan Berlin received the two letters that George Berlin wrote from Monterey and Richmond in mid-June, but after that none of his letter got through for a long time.[18] The Northern troops, Susan reported to George from Buckhannon at the beginning of July, "all that I have met with yet is very polite and gentlemanly they have treated me very kindly so far."[19] Westfall recorded in his diary on July 22 that George Berlin had returned to Buckhannon, but if he did it was for a very short stay.[20] It is more likely that Westfall was mistaken or had intended to write that Frederick Berlin had returned from another trip to the oil fields or that Susan Berlin had returned. She spent part of the time between the second week of July and the first part of September with her parents in Philippi, but she went back and forth more than once.

Outside of Buckhannon, where neither army was in control, a species of terror reigned. South of town in the little community of French Creek—known as little Massachusetts for its notorious Unionism,[21] and where ten men voted for Frémont in 1856—Marcia Louise Sumner Phillips was worried. A distant relation of Massachusetts senator Charles Sumner and wife of a captain in the county militia who remained loyal to the United States, she heard rumors and news that frightened her. In her diary for June 27, she wrote, "A day of terror and alarm to most of French Creek." The next day was "another exciting day," and the day after that abounded with "a great many rumors." On the last day of June she rejoiced to hear that several thousand Northern troops were en route to Buckhannon and that they had seized "400 rebels."[22]

Unionist Marcia Phillips went into Buckhannon on the Fourth of July, where as many as 13,000 soldiers were reportedly present. The army and its local supporters held a big, patriotic parade, celebrating and firing thirty-six rounds of artillery, one for each of the states, the states still in the Union and the states trying to get out.[23] Secessionist Susan Berlin saw it, too, and complimented the "very good band of music" that performed in the parade.[24] After the parade, the Union soldiers retired to their tents, loosened their hot uniforms, and relaxed. One of the volunteers wrote in his diary that throughout the camp soldiers were singing in their tents, some "'Dixie' at the top of their voices" and some "The Star Spangled Banner." The popular song "Dixie" had not yet become so identified with the Confederate cause as it did later, and at that time scarcely anybody would have thought it odd that Ohio and Indiana soldiers were singing "Dixie" in Virginia. The divisions between Northerners and Southerners, between Unionists and Confederates, were not yet as wide as they would very soon be or as enduring. Besides, the soldier wrote, "'The Star Spangled Banner' is being executed so horribly that even a secessionist ought to pity the poor tune."[25]

General George B. McClellan arrived in Buckhannon a few days later with several hundred more men and made the town his temporary headquarters.[26] Vocal supporters of the Confederacy suddenly became very scarce. As Susan wrote, "all the Secession men have left town I believe excepting those that have taken the oath there is but very few that have not taken the oath."[27] That is to say, many of George Berlin's new political allies, those who had applauded his speech in the courthouse, had taken an oath of allegiance to the United States or had left town, stranding Susan Berlin and their children without much friendly protection.

McClellan also wrote about the disappearance of secessionist sentiment in Buckhannon and Upshur County. "We are welcomed wherever our men go," he reported. "It is wonderful to see how rapidly the minds of many of these people become enlightened when they find we can protect them. Fear and ignorance combined have made most of the converts to secession; the reverse process is now going on with great rapidity."[28] A Northern private recorded something similar. "Many of them say they were deceived," he wrote, "and entered the service because they were led to believe that the Northern army would confiscate their property, liberate their slaves, and play the devil generally. As they thought this was true, there was nothing left for them to do but to take up arms and defend themselves."[29] He was probably correct. Susan Berlin had written something similar in her letters in April. Southerners' misunderstandings of the motivations of Lincoln and the Republicans no doubt contributed to many of them becoming Confederates, as Susan Berlin did; and Lincoln's misunderstandings about the attitudes of Southerners may have made matters even worse.[30]

Some men who remained secessionists melted into the mountains and began an irregular guerilla war. Some fled. Some joined the Confederate army. From day to day it was not clear who was in control in any particular place. A Union soldier on duty in the northern part of the county wrote in his diary for July 8: "The few Union men of this section have, for weeks past, been hiding away in the hills. Now the secessionists have taken to the woods. The utmost bitterness of feeling exists between the two. A man was found to-day, within a half mile of this camp, with his head cut off and entrails ripped out, probably a Union man who had been hounded down and killed."[31]

Some of the women who sided with the Confederacy boldly maintained their conspicuous presence in Buckhannon and in the surrounding counties. At the end of July in nearby Weston, Colonel Rutherford B. Hayes distinguished between the behavior of the women and the men who supported secession, writing, "the women avow it openly because they are safe in doing so, but the men are merely sour and suspicious and silent."[32] Throughout the summer in the mountains of northwestern

Virginia, Hayes and other men reported on bushwhackers attacking and annoying the United States Army. "The Union men here hate and fear them,"[33] Hayes wrote. "Persecutions are common, killings not rare, robberies an every-day occurrence. The war brings out the good and evil of Virginia. Some of the best and some of the worst characters I ever heard of, have come under our notice."[34]

During that time of uncertainty and fear, Susan Berlin and her unmarried sisters Elizabeth and Margaret tried and failed to obtain permission from the army to join George Berlin in the east.[35] "I have a good deal to tell you when I see you," Susan wrote on July 5. "I do not know when that will be but I do not want them to touch a hair of my sweet man's head for the world, he is mity sweet." She wanted him to return soon. "I hope so at lest, you know best what to do about comeing home. I am very much distressed about you indeed. I think it is very hard that You have to be separated from us so long. I do hope to heavens they will make peace for I am sick and tired of this fuss." She signed her first letter to her husband after he left home again, "Yours Affectionately" and added half a dozen cross-mark kisses to her signature.[36]

About a week after the big Fourth of July parade, Susan and the children went to Philippi to stay with her parents. They spent much of the summer there, until the middle of September. She left Frank in Buckhannon to earn her some money by hauling freight in Berlin's wagon.[37] Much of the language of fear was going out of her letters as she took charge of everything during her husband's second absence. She also worried about her two younger brothers, Charles A. Holt and William F. Holt (also called Will or Ferd). Charles was in school at Virginia Military Institute and later was one of the famous New Market Cadets.[38] George Berlin knew, or had heard, that they were serving in one of the volunteer units of the new Confederacy in Randolph County.[39] Susan bought clothing for the children, reported on the death of a horse that George had recently purchased, and prepared to get the family's affairs in order so that when an opportunity became available she could join her husband. "I wish you would let me know," she wrote him, "whether you would like for us to come to Dixey or not."[40]

Although some of the tension and fear were going out of Susan's letters, there was still much about which to be tense and afraid. The United States Army began arresting men suspected of aiding the Confederacy.[41] Susan heard that George's opponent in the February election, secessionist lawyer John S. Fisher, was arrested at the end of the summer and sent to Ohio.[42] Frightening rumors circulated almost daily, and Confederate sympathizers fully expected to have their property confiscated and sold.

Susan wrote George in the middle of July about the boldness of some of their hometown women. She told him a story that Richmond newspapers later repeated, that two women and the daughter of one of them had been arrested in Buckhannon. One of the trio, according to what she heard, had cut a telegraph wire and stuck the loose ends in the ground. Army officers asked why she did that, and "she said she wanted them to hear from their friends in Hell & wanted to find out whether there was room for any more Yankees in that place."[43] Virginia native and lifelong resident Susan Berlin approved and had become as committed to the Confederate cause as was her immigrant husband, George Berlin.

Susan continued to have nightmares and dreams about George's death. She told him about one of them. "I was the most miserable being on earth," she wrote, "I thought it would kill me until I wakened up and found it all a dream. Oh, how glad I was when I waked up. I was going on at a dreadful rate when I woke up." She also asked about her brothers Charles and Ferd. She worried about them, too. "Write to me soon for the Lords sake and tell me all the news."[44]

George and Susan were unable to arrange for her to join him in "Dixey." She remained in the west where relationships between Union and Confederate sympathizers deteriorated. Her old friends in Buckhannon who remained loyal to the Union were not helpful to her, and she began to criticize some of them. Edward J. Colerider, for instance, one of the town's leading merchants and a former mayor, remained a firm Union man. He employed a cobbler and had promised to provide the Berlin children with new shoes before the winter. Susan complained to her husband about Colerider. "I told you I did not believe he would make them when you left I told you so. he has told one dozen lies about them. I do not believe he intends to make any." With one or two exceptions, she concluded, "There is no person in Buchanan what will do the least favor for me."[45]

By the autumn she also began to doubt the wisdom of his trying to get back home. The army had arrested more Confederate sympathizers and sent them to Columbus, Ohio, where nobody knew what would become of them. Certainly, George would suffer the same fate or worse. Susan was feeling victimized, too. She wrote her husband that she had sold to the army some of the brick and stone that he had purchased the preceding year for the new house because "if I had not let them have them they would have taken them without paying for them."[46]

In spite of living with the threat of war all around, other aspects of life, like shoes for the children, had to be taken care of, and Susan Berlin took care of them. She reported to George on the children's health—mumps and bad colds—and her own—she was plagued with a cough and fever off and on all the next winter. She also wrote him about a cloudburst that flooded Buckhannon late in September and how his brother, in order to save the piano that George had recently purchased for her, had moved it upstairs in his own house, out of the reach of the high water.[47] She also reported that after secessionists were expelled from local offices under a resolution adopted at one of the Wheeling conventions, Frederick Berlin had run for commonwealth's attorney (George Berlin's old office) for the district that included Upshur and Barbour Counties, but he lost to another staunch Union man, Nathan Taft, of Philippi.[48] During the autumn she contemplated moving back to Philippi for the winter and living in an old house that her father owned, rather than staying in Buckhannon and paying high rent to live in a house with a smoky chimney and without reliable neighbors for support. Susan Berlin was an exile already, evicted from her own house in town.[49]

The consequences of the Civil War were becoming evident in many ways. Late in the spring of 1861 in Hampton Roads, in eastern Virginia, enslaved people began taking advantage of the war and freed themselves by seeking refuge with the United States Army. They were not the only ones. In September, Susan complained about the enslaved man George had hired to work for him for the year 1861. "Frank thinks that he is free now and does not do any thing half his time. since the troops came in he has not been the same negro that he was before."[50]

Her father's twenty-six-year-old enslaved man Milt, or Mit, took an even bolder step. He escaped from slavery and went to Ohio, where he had the additional boldness to write a letter to a member of his former owner's family. Holt asked a magistrate to request the governor of Ohio to have the man secured and returned, but that was the last time that the family ever heard of him. Nobody recorded whether Milt took with him the young enslaved woman and baby whom Thomas Holt also owned.[51] Perhaps he did; perhaps he did not and decided to leave behind everything about his life in slavery when he fled.

"Milt is among the things that were," wrote Susan's friend and relative by marriage, Isabella Neeson Woods. She was wife of George's convention colleague Samuel Woods, who was the brother of Stephen Holt's widow. She was the mother of the baby who had died in the spring soon after Stephen's death. She had an early and poignant realization that regardless of what happened that autumn or when the war concluded, their world would never be the same again, slavery included. "Milt is among the things that were," she wrote sadly.[52]

Because of his notorious conversion to the Confederate cause, George Berlin was unable to secure safe passage through the lines and return home, and Susan Berlin was unable to secure safe passage through the lines to join him. As his second absence from home grew longer and longer, her loneliness grew worse. ("I want to see you so much. I think of you most all the time and dream about you every night nearly."[53]) They could no longer exchange letters through the United States mail, nor did they have many safe opportunities to send letters back and forth through the lines and across the mountains.[54] None of his letters written between the middle of June 1861 and the middle of January 1862 survive, and at least some never reached her. Early in October one of their acquaintances returned from eastern Virginia carrying a letter that George sent to Susan, but he did not deliver it. Here is how she reported to her husband on how she had taxed the man about his failure to bring her a letter: "he toled me he was afraid to bring a letter for me. he said you wanted him to bring one but I toled him I know he did bring one from you and threw it away for fear of being caught with letter's and he laughed and sayed he did bring one part of the way and threw it away. he brought some other letters for different persons and distroyed them but I cannot blame him. I suppose he was scared all the time for fear of being taken."[55]

"We are getting along tolerably well," Susan reassured George late in September; "do not make yourself miserable on our account we will do the best we can untill you get back. so dont be uneasy about us." She rented her wagon and the services of the no-longer-reliable Frank to a man she trusted in order to earn some money. If she did not have to sell the wagon to support her family, if she could afford to keep the wagon, perhaps she could combine resources with Isabella Woods or some other friend (some other friend of the Confederate cause) who had a second horse to make up a team so that they could to go and meet their husbands.[56]

Susan continued having difficulty collecting money George was owed and still had difficulty fending off people posing as his creditors. She lacked access to his accounts and effective means of defending her own interests. One man who owed George money could not be made to pay: "one day he came," she wrote, "but went as he came and never has paid me yet nor never will as long as you are not here to make him. he knows that a woman cannot do as a man can."[57] About an application from a man who claimed George owed him money for the piano Susan wrote, "I was obliged to give it up or let it be sold for Debt as they talk of takeing all the absent Secesh's Property and pay their Debts but do not be uneasy," she tried to reassure her husband; "we will get along some how untill you get back. Providence allways provides."[58] Another man even asked her whether she would sell his law books, a collection that he prized, as if the local people no longer expected him to return home and resume his practice.[59]

"I got 70 dollars for brick and rock from the Northern people to build bake ovens and foundations," Susan reported in a matter-of-fact way late in October, bringing up to date the tale of the wastage of his building materials for the new house, "but they have Stolen all the plank nearly on the Island. they took a good deal of corn and all of the vegatables, except a few pumpkins and a few cabbages. they took the best of all the things, I have only two or three pumpkins now left at the house. I have a few potatoes left. they took nearly all of them before they got big anough to eat. I had not used any of them. we have about six bushels of them left I suppose."[60]

As was the case with many other people, the war brought out some unpleasant aspects of Susan Berlin's character. Her exasperation increased and with it her criticism of old friends and even of family members. Colerider had still not supplied the children's shoes by the end of October, and it was beginning to get cold. She complained to George that "he has told anough lies to send him to the Devil long ago without telling any more." After some of their Unionist friends assured her that George would be safe if he returned to Buckhannon, Susan told him not to come back: "I would rather you would stay where you are than to trust yourself to the Union men of this part of the Country. they make out they would be so glad to see you and sign a petition to get you back but I cannot put any confidence in them at all about anything. they are a hundred times worse than the Northern men."[61]

And Susan got suspicious of Frederick Berlin, George's brother, George's oldest and closest friend, whom she accused of keeping some money that George had sent to him for her. In one letter at the end of October she three times accused Frederick of dishonesty, and she repeated her accusations again in January.[62] She also warned George about trusting his brother's political judgment. "I do not care what Fred tells you do not believe him. he just wants to get you here and if he meets you any where he will persuade you to come back here and he believes the liars here. they will pretend to protect you untill they get you here like they do all that come and then they will take you right off to Columbus and then you may never get back here again. They might hang you for all we know. no do not place yourself in their power is the advice your wife will give you. do not listen to Fred. you know what I allways told you about him he will do all for his own interests. you know he will not do any thing only to his own interest. I cannot get much out of him at any rate."[63]

The Civil War had terrible effects on many families, not only on the families that had fathers or husbands or sons or brothers in the army, but also on the families that were divided, as were many in the divided border commonwealth of Virginia and in its divided border counties. The uncertainties of the times and the delay, or inability, to get messages through the lines bred suspicions and made matters worse, even if there were little or no grounds for suspicions of the kind that Susan developed about Frederick and that she cultivated for several months during that first winter of the war.[64] The tone of fear and tension had gone out of Susan Berlin's letters, but fear and tension expressed themselves in her conduct. She became more suspicions and judgmental. Holding her family together was stressful, and her complaints about her brother-in-law showed it.

At Christmas, his year having expired, "old Frank" left, and Susan suddenly had "no person to haul coal. we have anough to last while I stay here and wood too as I made him cut anough to last awhile before we went. he refuses to be hired out he says. he is agoing to do for himself."[65] And that was the last that Susan or George Berlin wrote about Frank, or Uncle Frank, or Frank Little, who had worked for them for several years, who had belonged to another white man, and who had decided, much like Milt, to seize the opportunity that the Civil War provided to live free. Frank decided that he was "agoing to do for himself."

In Buckhannon, where Susan Berlin remained from September 1861 until February 1862, she and her family daily saw evidences of the divided nature of their hometown. Union troops were stationed there off and on during the winter, as they moved from place to place in anticipation of Confederate troop movements. When the army was in town, it held parades in the street right outside of the house that she rented in October when she moved back to Buckhannon; soldiers lined up in the street to receive their pay; they held parties in the street; they were visible everywhere.[66] Sometimes, in order to repay the soldiers in their own coin, "Secesh" women marched up and down the streets, too.[67]

On special occasions like Christmas Eve, the divisions were even more apparent. Civilian Unionists, the women especially, paraded through the town, announcing their political allegiance. "Secesh" women, perhaps including Susan and some of her sisters, too, did the same. Even African American women, some perhaps free, some perhaps still enslaved, put on their finery and used the public streets to demonstrate their own independent identities and political allegiances.[68]

Susan Berlin celebrated Christmas without her husband in 1861 in the house she had rented at the corner of Main and Springs Streets from Sylvester B. Phillips and lived there with her children and Hulda, her younger sister, who was still serving as domestic servant to the household.[69] Sometimes her other sisters, Elizabeth and Margaret, were also there. Her new landlord, a captain of one of the Union companies, was the husband of Marcia Phillips, the French Creek diarist. An uneasy civility was still sometimes possible between civilians on opposite sides of the conflict, even between Marcia Phillips and Susan Berlin, although in her private diary Phillips did not conceal her disapproval of the politics of the secessionists.

Marcia Phillips was also in town for Christmas Day and reported that "everybody is on the street today. The *colored ladies* are flitting around in the gayest apparel and giving themselves such exquisite airs. The Secesh ladies are out too, sweeping the pavement with their silk dresses."[70] She did not state whether Susan Berlin and any of her sisters were on parade that Christmas Day. They might have been. They certainly made no secret of their politics, even though they must have known that among the men of the county secession spirit had disappeared or disappeared with them.

The leading secessionist men were by then almost all gone—permanently gone, in most instances, although that was not yet foreseeable—and within a year and a half Upshur County would become part of the new loyal state of West Virginia. An April 1862 referendum on the new state's first constitution won approval in the county by a vote of 719 to 2, according to Westfall, and in a separate referendum at the same time on adding to it a gradual emancipation provision, 594 of the county's voters approved and only 13 disapproved.[71] Among the men who remained in Upshur County, defenders of slavery and advocates of secession became things of the past. Among the men who left to join one of the two armies, men who joined the United States Army outnumbered men who joined the Confederate army ten to one.[72] One effect of the war was that Upshur County, once reliably Democratic on election day, became for the remainder of the century even more reliably Republican.[73]

Two days after Christmas, Susan had a party in her rented house. She and Hulda invited her landlord and landlady, who brought along Captain Moses S. Hall, commander of a Union company from Ritchie County. They all spent the evening with the Berlin family "to take a little Christmas with them," as Marcia Phillips recorded in her diary. She did not record whether she took along some leftover tipsy-cake, a sponge cake soaked in brandy with eggnog poured over it.[74] If she knew about George Berlin's attitude toward alcohol, she probably did not. Marcia Phillips wrote a brief account of the party in her old house in town where Susan Berlin and her sisters and children were residing. "Mrs. B's situation is not a pleasant one," Phillips wrote. "She and her sisters are all Secesh and wish to leave town and to go East Va. but the U. S. officers will not let them have a pass, fearing that they might carry information to the enemy. Berlin is in Eastern Va. and is not allowed to come back."[75]

Other "Secesh" women were also stranded in Buckhannon, and their lot was not often easy, but the women in Susan Berlin's household nevertheless had a jolly Christmas party in spite of, or in order to spite, their predicament. They sang popular songs, running through all their favorites and eventually coming down to "Dixie." Hulda volunteered to sing that song, as Phillips described the offer, "if it would not make us angry."

Perhaps not realizing that by the end of 1861 the song was becoming more of a sectional anthem than it had been in the summer, they "assured her of our amicable feelings." Marcia Phillips, as patriotic a Unionist as any man or any other woman in the county, had herself sung the song as recently as October, but Hulda Diddle sang new verses that openly celebrated the Confederacy.[76] She "commenced in a shrill, clear voice," Phillips wrote in her diary, and sang with gusto, not failing to stress "the defeat at Manassas and how the *Yankees* fled, and praised up General Lee and Beauregard, in an aggravating manner." The trio of Unionists got very nervous, perhaps fearing that somebody outside would hear and know that they were inside with the lusty singer of a rebel song. They tried to remain polite. "Capt. Hall and Capt. P—— hemmed and coughed and twisted about in their chairs," Marcia Phillips recorded, "and laughed and the lady kept on, 'louder yet, and yet more shrill' giving most theatrical flourishes, and seeming to enter into it, with her whole soul." Hall and Marcia Phillips coughed loudly and repeatedly to cover up their discomfort, but Captain Phillips "bore it more patiently than the rest of us."[77]

Susan Berlin and her family made the best of their situation that winter in Buckhannon. She managed as much of George's business as she could, Hulda kept house for the family, and her sisters Elizabeth and Margaret often stopped by to visit or play cards. At the New Year, Maria—Susan's sister, Frederick's wife—spent the day with them, and they all spent the next day at Maria's. Captain Phillips stopped by, as he occasionally did. A few days later he came by again to tell Susan that he had learned that George was on the way back to Buckhannon, but she did not believe it and wrote him to reassure him of her commitment to him and to the Confederate cause. "I said I knew you were not comeing without the southern army was before you."[78]

Susan's predicament naturally made George angry because his old friends had treated her shabbily. Isabella Woods recorded at the beginning of 1862 that "Old Mrs. Holt"—Susan's mother—"told me that Mrs. Susan Berlin would not be allowed to move or sell any persons property in Buccannan."[79] The occasional letters from Susan that George received gave him consolation, because he learned that she was still alive and well, but they made him angry, too. Reading the letters that she wrote after the New Year parties (only one of two survives), he replied, "I was still more rejoiced to learn that you are all living & well & that you have not been as yet driven out of the house by my *friends*. They seem to have acted bad enough but I do not feel disappointed, for men are the vilest brutes (as a general thing) that crawl or creep on the face of the Earth &

I was fearful that when they found that they could do so with impunity, they would plunder & abuse my family in my absence, & all that I hoped was that you would find a shelter some where until the storm is over or until I can reach you or you me. But for heaven's sake do not fret yourself about it, take it coolly & be as contented as a phylosopher, for I assure you that time will make all things right, and be farther assured that I have plenty here & elsewhere & shall have an ample living if they destroy & steal all I have in Western Va, all I desire is to have you & the children comfortable & happy & improving yourselves until we meet again."[80]

He also tried to dispel her suspicions about his brother's behavior, for "if I can't trust my Brother who could I trust. He may say many wild things & apparently do wrong some times, but in the end you will find all things right. I know what I have & I will know who gets it, & hold him who receives it responsible. . . . I have written a long letter to Brother which I want you to read as a more complete answer to your letter. I had not time to write the same things to both of you, as my explanations are very long, neither was it necessary when you live so close together."[81]

George sent Susan instructions about how to protect herself and their property, "as my creditors seem disposed to act the dog & like brutes." He gave her citations to sections of the legal code that she could look up in his law books or that Frederick could find in his own law books to secure their property from illegitimate claims or confiscation. "Dont admit to any one that you have money. get all you can & give Brother Receipts for what he pays you. there are no liens on my property. give up no money received or which you may yet receive from any one either to officers or any one else. you & Brother must sell all you can. make a belt & put your money in it & sew it around you but dont loose it."[82] Later in the spring he repeated his advice and his determination: "I know too much law for such contemptable thieves & scounderals & those who buy me for a fool will loose their money in the end. I know what I am doing. I know my rights & how to assert and maintain them, and so long as the war lasts my remedy will continue & for years thereafter, & therefore I pray you not to be uneasy & allow yourself to be distressed about such trespasses."[83]

Except when Berlin attended the second session of the convention in Richmond in June 1861 and the third session in November and December, his whereabouts for the remainder of the year are not well documented. After the Battle of Rich Mountain in July, he returned as far east as Monterey in Highland County, where in August 1861 wrote a letter to General Robert E. Lee. He introduced himself by reminding the general that they had met when he took command of the Virginia army during the first session of the convention back in April, "I being then, as now, an humble member of that body from the County of Upshur." Berlin urged the general to expedite the transfer of military resources to western Virginia to protect the region from Northern invasion. He repeated the essence of the argument about the defenseless condition of the west that he wrote about during the spring in the draft speech that he did not make to the convention.

By then, the Wheeling conventions had moved the western counties well down the road to separation from the eastern counties. The delegates had declared that all the state offices in Virginia were vacant and had elected a new governor and sent two men to Washington to fill the state's vacated seats in the United States Senate. Berlin asked General Lee to protect the Confederate sympathizers, if possible, without alienating the loyal Union men. "While all admit," he explained, "that the leaders of the rebellion against the State & those citizens who prompted & aided in the arrest & mistreatment of the Secessionists in N: W. Va, and such as voluntarily acted as spies for the enemy should be severely dealt with, great caution should be exercised in dealing with & disposing of such men for if we give too great latitude to arrests and indulge in too much severity in our treatment of these misguided Unionists, it will result in driving thousands of them into the ranks of the Northern army, who would otherwise remain neutral, or soon come to our aid."[84]

Berlin went back to Richmond in November for the third session of the convention, but it is not clear where he spent much of the autumn of 1861. He probably returned to the western army during the early part of the winter, as he had done during the recess. If so, he was not near any serious fighting, but he may have been exposed to some physical hardships. Wherever he was, he thought about his future, and by the end of the year he had abandoned the idea that he could return safely home to Buckhannon. He began to think about a new future for himself and his family. He and his father-in-law, Thomas Holt, of Barbour County, completed arrangements to exchange some of Berlin's western land holdings for Holt's property in Augusta County. It is possible that Henry Westfall and Frederick Berlin, who did paper work together for two days at the end of December and three days during the first week of January, were preparing some of the necessary deeds and conveyances.[85]

Holt still owned the land in Alabama, and Berlin went down there in March 1862 to make certain that it would not be sold for nonpayment of taxes. He paid the taxes and bought some property for himself, thinking that it might be wise to move from the cold and rugged mountains of western Virginia to the warmer climate and gentler rolling hills of northwestern Alabama. The farmland there was certainly far superior to anything in western Virginia. "I was much better pleased with Alabama this time than before," he wrote to Susan after he returned to Virginia late in March. "It is not only a beautiful Country but possesses Church, Educational & agricultural, universal & commercial advantages & facilities so infinitely superior to those of Northwestern Virginia that there is no comparison between them. I think you would like the Country exceedingly well. You shall at least have an opportunity to see it if we ever met again. The fine fruit & mellons I know would be delicious and attractive to the Children, and the boys would be delighted with the large quantity of fish in the streams & game in the fields."[86]

Almost ten months, by then, they had been separated, by far the longest separation since they had met, much longer than any of her lying-in absences in Augusta County while he tried to make a living for his new family. He was still as lonely as ever. "My heart aches when I think of you," George wrote after he returned to Virginia from Alabama, "& that is every hour of the day. Oh what a wretched time I have spent since I saw you last although I have tried & thought of every thing imaginable to occupy my mind & keep me from thinking of home & the dear ones there, but my dear Sue & my dear children hourly pass in review before my minds eye & often momentarily occupy my thoughts, there is no rest for me away from you, my heart is aching forever. Oh what would I not give to have you with me? What honorable act would I not perform to enjoy the sweet society of you my dear and of our children?"[87]

So much did George miss his family that he actually felt guilty to be enjoying better health during the winter of 1861–62 than he had in years. When the anniversary of their marriage came around again on the last day of March 1862, he wrote another love letter to Susan, but not so sweet a letter as on the previous anniversary, in that letter from Richmond that deeply moved his lonely wife. "This is the 16th anniversary of our marriage & therefore I hail it with delight because of the many happy years of pleasure & happiness with you, which it has secured to me, and I sincerely hope & pray that we may spend many more gay & happy days & years together & that it will be so I have no doubt it if we do not forget each other & ourselves and as there is no fickleness and no coldness in my nature & as my love for you is as constant & as true as the needle to the pole you have nothing to fear on my part though years should separate us, & therefore I hope you will not forget me & allow some Yankee to carry you off, and as people have always been disposed to slander you most unjustly I hope you will give their vile tongues no chance to injure you. But you have always been so good & true & having reached the years of discretion I feel as if I have nothing to apprehend & that you are safe, & in this belief I feel happy & pray for the speedy return of the day which will bring us together again."[88]

Susan Berlin moved back to Philippi in February to live with her parents, taking her unmarried sisters and as much of their household possessions with her as she could. "A great many of the Secesh residents of Buckhannon came to call and sympathize with Mrs. Berlin before she left," Marcia Phillips recorded in her diary.[89] Susan Berlin went to Philippi to be with her family, not because it was safer there. In fact, Barbour County was more deeply divided than Upshur County. Almost two thirds of Barbour County's soldiers fought for the United States, more than one-third for the Confederate States.[90]

Not one of the letters that Susan wrote to her husband between the beginning of January and the middle of June 1862 has survived, and there is very little in the texts of his remaining letters to indicate precisely how she fared during that time. They lost control of all their property in Upshur County and feared that they would lose everything else. "Box up & hide my books save them if you possably can," he advised her at the end of March. "They could be hid away at Jane's"—at the house of Jane Woods Holt, widow of Susan's brother Stephen—"or in the hay mow or such place"; but Susan had already hidden them someplace else.[91]

After spending time in Monterey, where other political refugees from northwestern Virginia first congregated, George settled temporarily in Staunton, where he had studied law in the mid-1840s.[92] He once again contemplated his future, as he had in that place back then, when he had decided to give up teaching school and to practice law and to marry Susan Holt. Residing in the Virginia Hotel in Staunton, he tried to console his wife from afar. Usually optimistic in spirit, Berlin took special pains to write hopeful letters to his wife, to reassure her that their separation was temporary and that when they were reunited they would again be happy. He tried to chase away dull care, as he liked to say.[93] He sometimes began with a jaunty, conversational, "Well my Dear Sue," and repeatedly reassured her of his devotion.

"I think of you every hour of the day," he wrote in April, "& wish as often that I was by your side within the sweet influance of your presence, basking in the sunshine of your radient smiles & charmed by your kind attentions & soothing caresses. When I look back upon the happy hours so sweetly spent with you & the happiness which I always enjoyed in your society it revives all the warm fresh feelings of my youth & causes me to wish to live that happy period over again. I know that we had our little troubles & vexations but I was always phylosophical anough to look upon them as necessary and unavoidable evils & had the same effect upon the social & domestic world as storms have upon the physical world, purifying in their effect, & cause the sun & every thing else to shine the warmer, brighter & more cheering in the social circle." Realizing that she reacted more emotionally to changing circumstances than he did, he tried to reassure her as often as possible and wrote, "allow nothing to trouble you & make you miserable, for it will do no good and only wear your dear life out."[94]

Berlin kept in touch with refugees from home, those still in Monterey and those who moved farther east to Staunton and the Valley of Virginia. From time to time another family made it through the lines, bringing news from home and sometimes letters, too. The trip was difficult even in good times, but during the winter and early in the spring it was more so, and military movements of the two armies added to the danger. One of their acquaintances from Buckhannon "got through to this side of the Mountains a few days ago," George wrote to Susan late in April, "but she had a hard time of it & it is really a wonder that it (the trip) did not kill her. I would not have you go through what she did for a thousand dollars, but she is safe now & well as could be expected after such a trip, journeying night & day through trackless forests & mountains, over rivers & swamps."

The news that George received informed him about how his family had been treated and his "property sacrificed &c, &c,." He wrote to reassure his wife late in April that he had access to ample financial resources to secure their future, and that he intended to settle accounts all around. "You shall be amply compensated for all you have suffered & my *Friends* amply rewarded for all they have done." That is, he would use his legal knowledge to settle the score with his quondam friends who had turned on him and his family after he had cast his lot with the Confederacy.[95]

Although no longer holding any public office—the convention to which he had been elected in February 1861 having ceased to exist in December—Berlin still worried about the welfare of his state and the fate of the western counties. The statehood movement in the west particularly upset him. He believed that his former convention colleagues who were leading the movement were acting against the wishes of the people of the region, and sometime that winter he wrote an article, or speech, to try to effect a reconciliation between east and west. Perhaps he wrote it for delivery in the third and final session of the convention when he was in Richmond in November and December.[96]

Berlin believed that the "majority of the people of Northwestern Virginia" who voted against secession in May 1861 "had no thought, or design of dividing the State, nor of placing themselves in an attitude of hostility against it, neither did they believe that by reason of such vote, they would be considered & treated as *enemies* of the State. They simply expressed their desire, a preference, as in all former elections & expected to be governed by the voice of the State & the masses so declared." Regardless of whether the deductions he drew about their attitudes were accurate, that is what he believed: "at this day I am assured through various & reliable channels of information that in consequence of the occurrances & developments to which I have alluded, there are far more Secessionists in Northwestern Virginia now than there were in May last & the number is daily increasing."

"But it is often asked," Berlin went on, "why did the people there not rush to arms and join their Southern friends when the decision of the State was made known? Simply because they had no arms to rush to & the enemy had already advanced & taken possession of the Country, & within 15 or 20 days after the election, had rushed forward & taken possession of the Mountain passes & blocked up every outlet from that section of the State, & hence it is that not one tenth of even the Secessionists of that section, willing & capable of bearing arms, have been enabled to join us, And as these people were then in the very midst of their planting season, they had no slaves to perform that labor for them (scarcely one tenth part of their population being slaves) it was unreasonable to expect all those who were disposed to stand by Virginia, to abandon their homes & families at the approach of the enemy & join the army east of the Mountains, considering the uncertainty of coming events & the apprehensions which oppressed those people."

Berlin also asked, "can we not make some allowance for their timidity, hesitancy, & failure in duty when there were no adequate means of defence within their reach in time to arrest the enemy in his rapid advance to the Mountains; & is it right to call every man who voted against the ordinance of Secession 'a union man' & treat him as an enemy for that reason alone?" He objected to "the miserable policy of plundering those men on account of their former Union Sentiments," having been, himself, a victim of what he believed was a like policy of the Unionists in Upshur County.

Berlin began or wrote other essays that winter, too, perhaps sorting out in his own mind the proper policies that Virginia should adopt, or that he should advocate, as the war dragged on, getting bloodier and bloodier all the time. He drafted an essay that one of his children later docketed, "Written upon the encroachment of Abolition." In it, Berlin repeated some of the arguments and phrases from the long draft speech that he prepared for, but did not deliver at, the convention in the spring of 1861. Berlin remained convinced that Northern fanaticism had brought about the secession crisis and caused the Civil War.[97] He also made some notes on the subject of guerrilla war, the greatest danger in the western portion of Virginia by the summer of 1862, greater even than getting caught in a battle between real armies.[98]

During the course of the war, armies encamped at Buckhannon at least a dozen times, and late in the summer of 1862 an engagement took place on the very edge of town. Susan Berlin had been living with her parents in Philippi since February and was not present to witness the event. Even when she was in the very presence of warfare, though, the tone of the few surviving letters that George and Susan Berlin wrote during 1862 is different from the tone of their letters of the previous spring. In the first months of 1861, they were miserable in their loneliness and worried about business affairs, about planting the garden and the fruit trees, about the new house and the education of the children. The year 1862 was very different, and although those subjects were still important, they lived their lives in a different context, in a new kind of normal, to which they nevertheless adapted. Strange as it may seem, their wartime letters display less unease for personal safety than their earlier letters when war was still a fearful possibility. The times changed, and so did they.

6 Reunion

IN MAY 1862, SUSAN BERLIN WAS FINALLY ABLE TO TRAVEL east to reunite with her husband. She traveled with her younger brother John E. Holt and her sons Augustus, Lee, and six-year-old Benjamin, so that they could resume their education under their father's supervision. There are no surviving letters describing her ride over the mountains from Philippi to Staunton or to indicate how long she remained there or what they talked about, although much can readily be imagined.

Following their brief reunion, Susan and her brother returned to Philippi,[1] and she began to prepare for taking the other children to Staunton as soon as possible. About a week after she reached Philippi, Susan wrote to George, a letter that he received and saved, describing the journey back. Her horse went lame, protracting the journey and risking permanent injury to a valuable animal. "I have been doctoring him all the time since he is getting better now. Pa had to take his shoe off." Reflecting the new and dangerous conditions in which they lived their lives then, Susan wrote, in the middle of a long letter about family affairs, business, the health of the children, and the health of the horse, a passage about wartime violence: "I suppose you heard of John Harmon being shot just the other side of Leonard Harmons the day after we passed there. I am very sorry of that as I believe he is a clever man. I believe they do not know who did it but suppose the Guerillas did it. I think he was a harmless man. it is a great pitty for his wife and Children. we stopped there as we came over to get him to shoe the horse but he was not at home and we had to get Isaac to shoe him next morning."

People adapted to or became accustomed to wartime violence and did the best that they could under the circumstances. That is what Susan Berlin did, concluding that letter with, "Some of the Officers were to see us to question us a few days after we came, but did not learn much from me."[2] When United States Army officers first arrived in Buckhannon in June 1861, their very presence had frightened her, and the prospect of being arrested or of losing her property disturbed her dreams. But not now. In June 1862 she reported matter-of-factly, almost proudly, that the officers had learned nothing from her.

Susan's letter to George of July 14, 1862—she dated it as from Buckhannon but drew a line through the name of her former hometown and instead wrote, "Phillippi July 14th"—is the most nearly routine letter in the surviving exchange of 1861–62 letters between husband and wife. "My Dear George," she began. "I was glad to receive a letter from you to day and very happy to hear that you were all getting along so well." She commiserated with him on an attack of boils and inquired after the boys who were with him and reported to him on the children who were with her. Their youngest child, Charles, "is cutting his teeth and has a bowel complaint." She told him about an invitation to take tea with Isabella Woods, about getting soaked in a rainstorm, about a budding romance in town, and about how much more at home she felt in Philippi then than she had earlier. "I am satisfide to stay untill you come. I am not tired yet but it seems like it has been two or three month's since I was at home."[3]

That letter of July 14, 1862, is also the only letter that either George or Susan Berlin wrote in which either mentioned attendance at a church service. In one of her first letters after he left for the convention, Susan wrote from Buckhannon about "a Presbyterian Meeting going on here now," but all that she had to say on the subject was that the minister conducting the service was "not as good looking as he was when he was here before," not even whether she attended.[4] Susan was in a church a few weeks later for the funeral of her brother Stephen, mentioning it to her husband only by way of explaining why she did not return home from Philippi to Buckhannon until three days after Stephen's death. The funeral sermon was too long: "they preached the sermon at the Church. Mr Malery preached it and that made it so late."[5] George never mentioned attending church all the time that he was in Richmond and writing weekly or oftener.

In those letters and others—the other surviving family letters from the 1840s and 1850s include none from her to him—George Berlin scarcely ever wrote anything even remotely touching the subject of religion. He made only one glancing reference to churches when cataloging the virtues of Alabama early in 1862.[6] In some of his letters and speech drafts he referred to providence or prayed that difficulties would be resolved, but those expressions could as easily have been stock tropes of language and not genuine religious expressions. Susan Berlin's occasional references to prayers are in the same vein. Only this once, in July 1862, did either of them mention going to church. Susan wrote, "Bet and Hulda and myself came down on Sunday to preaching and went home in the evening and got such a soaking going home we liked to have ruined our bonnets. it poured down on us. we got wet to our skin."

Was attending "preaching" so routine a thing to do that neither mentioned doing so any more than they mentioned eating at mealtime or wearing a coat in cold weather? All around them they had opportunities to attend religious services, in Richmond when he was attending the convention, as well as in Buckhannon where they had lived and she remained most of the time until February 1862. In 1860, more than a dozen clergymen lived in Upshur County, mostly Baptists but a few Methodists, two ministers of the Church of the Brethren, and one Presbyterian.[7] The Presbyterian Church was adjacent to land that Berlin owned in Buckhannon, but the church's fragmentary surviving records do not disclose that they were members.[8] George Berlin had been baptized a Lutheran in Pennsylvania,[9] but his letters do not indicate whether he continued to regard himself as a Lutheran in the 1850s and 1860s, and no Lutheran clergyman resided in Upshur County at the time the Civil War broke out. The Holt family's religious affiliations, if any, are not known, either.

Still, it is surprising that this husband and wife did not tell each other about attending church or mention praying for the safety of the other or for the health and safety of the children. She did not write about the children saying their prayers, and he did not ask. Perhaps their religious beliefs and practices did not occupy a particularly central place in their personal and married lives.

Back when Berlin was a young and active member of the Sons of Temperance, and later, too, he took note of the importance of churches and religion in people's lives, and in some of his wartime ruminations on the parlous state of his country he singled out the divisions about slavery within the Protestant churches as one of the conspicuous evidences of the ruinous work of Northern antislavery fanatics. The absence of religious topics and themes from their private epistolary conversation and from his draft speeches suggests that for them religion was not then a frequent preoccupation or even an essential element of their lives.

Whether in that they were more typical or atypical is hard to say. Certainly, in the antebellum South, churches were vitally important social institutions, and religious beliefs and practices were important and frequent topics of conversation and correspondence. Religious revivals were a characteristic feature of the age. They took place in Buckhannon. Henry Westfall had recorded in his diary on January 26, 1861, that a big meeting commenced in town that day. He did not state what kind of meeting, but it lasted at least two weeks, as a religious revival would, not concluding until after Berlin won election to the convention.[10] Susan Berlin mentioned the Presbyterian revival later in the winter. Revivals enlivened religious beliefs and practices that had either gone dormant or burned less brightly between revivals. How or why George and Susan Berlin were, or appeared to be, substantially unfazed or uninvolved in their religious faith during their trials of 1861 and 1862 is not clear. It may be that letters and records documenting their religious affiliations, beliefs, and practices for that time simply do not exist. Perhaps they knew each other so well that they did not think that they needed to mention those subjects. Later, George was an elder in the Presbyterian church, and their sons Augustus, before he moved to California, and

Charles were deacons.[11] Sometimes silences mean as much or more than words, but in this instance the silence in their letters is more puzzling than instructive.

In any event, George and Susan Berlin had immediate and practical problems to discuss in their letters. They began to make arrangements for her to join him permanently in Staunton. Once, late in August 1862, he rode as far west as the mouth of Seneca Creek, in Pendleton County, in hope of meeting her en route, but she was not there. He promised to ride west again in his fancy new carriage to meet her and carry her back with him to old Virginia. They discussed where on the road to meet.[12]

Berlin had finally decided to make his home in the Shenandoah Valley of Virginia, not to try to return to Upshur County and not to move to Alabama. He rented the Lebanon White Sulphur Spring Hotel in Augusta County and proposed to set himself up as a hotelkeeper. He must have thought that he could rent rooms to refugees from the west if the usual travelers and holiday visitors from the east did not fill all his rooms. On August 23, he sent Susan a long list of eating utensils and bedding that he needed and that if possible she should pack in her wagon before leaving Philippi for the last time. If she could rent some additional horses and another wagon to carry it all, he promised to guarantee their safe return to the owners.

George Berlin had cut his ties with the west, where he had lived for fifteen years, and was starting over in the Shenandoah Valley, where he had once taught school, studied law, and married Susan Holt. He appeared to be optimistic about the future, genuinely optimistic, not the sometimes forced hopefulness of the letters early in their long separation when she needed reassurance. Their impending reunion was more assurance than any letter could supply. The only uneasiness he expressed was at a rumor that his brother, who continued to be opposed to secession, and who had tried to lure him back to Upshur County when it still was not safe, that Frederick wanted to join the United States Army. George explained to Susan that under the law of Virginia at that time, Frederick "jeopardizes his life & all his property." George instructed Susan to "tell your father to prevaile on him to abandon his foolish possi-tion."[13]

"Oh I was near forgetting," George then wrote, starting the final para-graph of the last of his surviving letters to Susan, "to tell you to bring at least a half bushel of salt with you if you can do so with convenience. could not some of your friends get a buggy & bring you part of the way as it will be so hard to ride in a wagon. You must at least get a gentle horse or two to ride part of the way. . . . Possible you could get all the horses you need from some of the secessionists who may wish to send horses over for sale, you could pretend & so could they that you purchased the horses & when you get here you could hand them over to any person they may designate. But come some way or other so that it be a safe & easy way, for I cannot stay away from my dear Sue any longer. Bring Huldah with you if you can & she wishes to come."[14]

There is one other letter in the file, the last surviving letter between George and Susan Berlin. She wrote to him from Philippi on September 19, 1862. It is also a rather routine letter about family affairs and quilt-ing bees and the like. "Ma is very kind in taeking care of little Charley for me. he crys sometimes in the night yet but not long. he often says he will tell Pa when any of them do anything to him he does not like." By then they had nearly completed their plans for her to move to Augusta County. He intended to go get her and escort her and the children and the supplies back to their new home. She was ready: "let me know when you can come for me. It will suit me any time that it suits you so let me know when you are comeing."[15]

Susan and George Berlin began their new life together, began again for the second time, in October 1862, when the United States Army fi-nally allowed her to take her other children east with her. The army did not allow him to go for them. Susan and George Berlin started their married lives all over again, but it was not easy. The scheme of running the hotel fell through, leaving Berlin in "an almost destitute condition, cut off from my property practice & friends & forced to make a living for myself and family as best I could."[16] He opened a mercantile store in

Middlebrook, a few miles south of Staunton, during the winter of 1862–63. Later in 1863 he applied for and received appointment as receiver of taxes in kind for the Confederate government, adding a few years to his age when making the application in order to persuade the secretary of war that he was too old for effective military service if drafted.[17] In that same year Berlin obtained a paying job as superintendent of the Staunton and Parkersburg Turnpike, which entitled him to an exemption from the state's conscription act, possibly because the new governor, who granted the exemption, believed that Berlin was forty-six years old, not thirty-nine.[18] Because much of the turnpike was in the loyal state of West Virginia and guarded by the United States Army, it is unlikely that he had much to do.[19]

George and Susan had another baby, a boy they named George Richard Berlin, born on August 26, 1863, less than ten months after their reunion. Susan had endured eight pregnancies and childbirths in seventeen years, all of them by the standards of the time risky, even dangerous, potentially life-threatening; and two of her babies had died. For about one-third of the time since Susan and George married, she had been pregnant or recovering from childbirth. The odds were probably against her, as they were against all of the women of her time, surviving that many closely spaced pregnancies. Susan's mother and her sister Maria both survived about the same number of pregnancies and childbirths. The women of the family must have been experienced and knowledgeable as well as physically resilient. They must have helped one another through the difficult times, including the especially difficult times when the babies did not survive as well as the difficult routine times that required her to tend a household with infants, toddlers, and fleet-footed little children who were all active at once. But this time, for the first time, Susan Berlin had her baby without the sympathetic ministering attendance of her mother or any of her sisters.

Because George and Susan were back together again, there are no letters that tell how they adjusted to their new life, how long they remained in Middlebrook, or where they may have gone to avoid the waves of warfare that swept through the Shenandoah Valley, impoverishing that rich breadbasket of the Confederacy. In 1864, he purchased a mill and other property on the bank of the North River near Bridgewater in Rockingham County, just north of the border with Augusta County, within a few miles of where Susan had grown up. In January 1865, Berlin wrote to his old Upshur County friend, Richard L. Brown, the man who had showed him around Washington four years earlier on his way to Richmond for the first time. Brown was still a Democrat and still optimistic about the chances for the Confederacy. He had spent most of the war in Richmond, where he received and read Berlin's letter, a letter that is lost. It gave Brown "the blues." Berlin asked him to help obtain equipment for the mill, and he also asked Brown to send him some hair dye. The passage of time or the pressure of the times was causing his hair, or Susan's hair, or both, to turn gray.[20]

Berlin resumed practicing law in the courts of Rockingham and the neighboring counties, finally reestablishing himself in his chosen profession. He had preserved his family in a time of danger. And the war finally ended. Their own sons were too young to fight, and they did not have to fear for their sons' safety or weep for their loss. Berlin took an oath of allegiance in the summer of 1865, becoming again a citizen of the United States and remaining, as he had always said he wanted to be, a citizen of Virginia.[21]

Susan and George Berlin looked forward to living happily ever after. Their extended family, on which she had relied and which they had assisted during the trying months of 1861 and 1862 and to which he was evidently deeply attached, was never again to be so close as it was before the war when they had all lived in the neighboring towns of Buckhannon and Philippi. The family began to disperse, partly as a consequence of the war—George and Susan Berlin were the first to leave their mountain home—and partly as a natural consequence of life in the nineteenth century. Children grew up and moved away; adults sought greener pastures. The Holt and Berlin family network grew smaller and became more scattered. Frederick Berlin never joined either army but remained a Union noncombatant, as George remained a Confederate noncombatant. Frederick and Maria Berlin and their children moved in 1870 to

Detroit, Michigan, where he dealt in real estate.[22] The sisters Elizabeth Holt and Margaret Holt remained in West Virginia, as their old home became known in 1863, and helped their parents. Susan's youngest sister Lucy and her brothers John and Ferd all died shortly after the war, all still in their twenties.[23] Their mother, Minerva Graham Holt, died in the autumn of 1869, and their father, Thomas Holt, in September 1872.[24]

Hulda had remained in the west, too, living in Philippi, and in 1865, about the time that the war ended in the east, she had a second son, whom she named Edgar. The extant family records do not disclose whether she was permanently reunited with her husband, but when Hulda—still not yet thirty years old—died at the beginning of 1869 and was buried in the cemetery in Philippi, she was identified as the wife of John Diddle.[25]

Two years after the end of the war, when prospects were improving and Susan's parents and Hulda were all still alive, Susan and George Berlin had another child, their ninth, a girl born on April 16, 1867. They named the baby for its mother. They named her Susan Miranda Berlin.

Susan Miranda Holt Berlin, the baby's mother and George Berlin's wife, died six days later, on April 22, of complications following the birth of her ninth baby. He buried her the next day in Woodbine Cemetery in Harrisonburg.[26] What George had feared and dreaded most during their many months of separation when the war began had actually come to pass. George and Susan were separated again. The bright eyes were closed forever.

7 | Regrets

Gᴇᴏʀɢᴇ ʙᴇʀʟɪɴ ʟɪᴠᴇᴅ ᴀʟᴍᴏsᴛ ᴛʜɪʀᴛʏ ᴍᴏʀᴇ ʏᴇᴀʀs, half again as long as he had already lived since he first met Susan Holt. He practiced law and in order to support his children invested in a variety of businesses. The winter after Susan died he laid off lots for a new town near where they had lived on the edge of Bridgewater. They called it Berlinton.[1] His mill was washed away in the great flood of October 1870, but he persevered and raised his children there in Berlinton, saw them educated and married, and served as an elder in the local Presbyterian Church. He owned an interest in a narrow-gauge railroad, and for a while he sold bone dust, a valuable fertilizing agent especially for vegetable gardeners like himself, eventually passing that business along to one of his sons.[2]

In 1874 Berlin went back to Buckhannon, perhaps for the first time since June 1861, to make a final settlement of all the outstanding property transactions in which he had been engaged, and perhaps to learn whether Thomas Holt's estate was sufficient for the maintenance of the few members of the family who still lived in Barbour County.[3] Berlin probably saw to it that none of Susan's remaining family there would be in want. Hulda's second son, Edgar Diddle, lived there in the capacity of a menial laborer until he died of typhoid fever in September 1888.[4] Although the name of her first son, George W. Diddle, appears only fleetingly in the county's public records, he may have remained there, too, through most or all of his life before dying of heart disease in January 1919.[5] If Hulda Diddle was the woman who had two daughters, as the census taker in 1860 recorded, neither the Berlin family records nor the public records indicate what happened to them, but they, too, probably died in infancy or childhood, as George and Susan's little Alice and William Lloyd had died.

George Berlin lived in Bridgewater for nearly thirty years after his wife died. He never remarried. He raised his children and educated them, and he wrote long essays on the value of education and perhaps delivered them to local literary societies or academies. In one of his surviving essays he wrote, "The wellfare, success & happiness of every condition & class of our people and the general safety of all" required proper education to preserve freedom and representative government, "so that the Dantons & Robespires, the Thad Stevensons & Beast Butlers of our Country cannot excite our people to madness and lead them & our Country to distruction."[6] Berlin continued to believe, as he stated often during 1861, that Northern fanatics had been responsible for the Civil War and for the ruin that it brought, and he believed after the war that Northern politicians continued to abuse the South. The destruction of the old South, which he had been powerless to prevent, and the consequent disruption of his family were not things that a man such as George Berlin could easily forget.

As his children grew into adulthood, some of them moved away. Three of his sons moved to California. The eldest, Frederick Augustus, followed his father into the law and moved to San Francisco. Charles, the last child born in Buckhannon, also moved to San Francisco (much as George and his brother Frederick had both moved to Staunton and then to Buckhannon), where he managed a furniture company. Benjamin became an attorney, too, and after practicing law for a time in Washington, D.C., he moved to Los Angeles in the 1880s to practice there. Berlin's two daughters married, and both moved to New York. Susan Miranda Berlin Scovil, whose birth led to Susan's death in 1867, died in New York City in the spring of 1895, not yet thirty, younger even than Hulda had been when she died. Emory Lee and George Richard (the first baby born following the end of George and Susan's long second separation) both remained in Bridgewater and became successful small town businessmen. Lee became secretary and treasurer of the Bridgewater Rolling Mills Company, and George editor and publisher of the local newspaper.

Perhaps feeling lonely, again, as his children were growing up, leaving home to attend school, and moving to distant cities, sometime in the 1880s George Berlin wrote a memorandum on the Berlin family's history.[7] The account begins with his paternal grandfather and is a fairly typical record of an American family of the nineteenth century. Some of his grandfather's children and some of the children of each succeeding generation died young and unmarried—just as had some of Susan's brothers and sisters, Hulda's son Edgar, and their own little Alice and William Lloyd—and some had grown up and moved west from their home in Pennsylvania to Indiana or, as was the case with George's own father, late in life all the way to Iowa. In each generation one or two children lived near their parents, but the others moved away and made their futures—but not necessarily their fortunes—elsewhere. Those moves meant in most instances that family members never saw one another again. In that, the members of the extended Berlin family shared some of the same experiences as millions of other Americans did between the birth of George's father in 1797 and George's own death in 1895.

George Berlin knew where his grandparents had lived and died, where his uncles and aunts had lived and died, where his cousins and some of their children lived, too. Family ties remained, although in many instances weakened by time and distance. By the time Berlin wrote his memorandum, members of the family lived or had lived in Pennsylvania, Ohio, and Indiana, in Virginia and West Virginia, and in Michigan, Iowa, Kansas, California, and New York.

Family ties revealed themselves in the names of the children. Given names had repeated among the sons and daughters of the Berlin family—George, Augustus, Frederick, Lee, Mary, Catherine (Kate)—and beginning with his and Frederick's marriages into the Holt family, given names from that family entered into and repeated in the Berlin family, too—Thomas, John, Stephen, Charles; Maria, Elizabeth, Margaret, Lucy, Susan. Some of his own children bore those family names; and Frederick and Maria's children had names that drew on the same family traditions. George wrote, "my brother Frederick practiced law some years in Phillippi & Buckhannon West Va.: but he is now in the Real estate business in Detroit Michigan, and his oldest son George H. is a druggist at Lapier, Michigan, and is married and has three children, his second daughter (Lucy) is also married to Mr Burrows and lives in that state. His 2d. son (Thomas) is also in Michigan, his oldest daughter (Kate) married Lewis Passmore of Philadelphia, and they are now living in Toledo Ohio, where her three brothers Frederick, John & Charley are also living & in business. Charley is going to school & F. & J. are in the foundary business."

Berlin wrote, too, about his other brother: "My Fathers youngest son Augustus is in Kansas now, having recently moved there from Story County, Iowa," where their father, sister, stepmother, and half-sister had lived and died. His children were named Eliza, Loretta, George, Thomas, and Frederick. George's sister Catharine (Kate) married before leaving Virginia and had three sons, whom she named Frederick, Lee, and Harry. His other two sisters, Amanda and Emeline, were by then dead, as was his half-sister Mary, his stepmother's "cub," whom he and Susan had not trusted.

Members of George Berlin's family had lived through many great events of American history and known the consequences of those events for their personal lives, as had he. The country fought three major wars during the decades that the family history memorandum covered and nearly a century of off-and-on conflict with Native American tribes. Political parties had been born, flourished, and died, including his own Whig Party. The industrial revolution and the building of the railroads had transformed the nation in many ways, as had the telegraph and many other revolutionary changes, none more revolutionary than the abolition of slavery as a consequence of the defeat of the Confederacy. Only once in the three closely written pages of the family history memorandum did Berlin mention any of those connections between the family's history and the nation's. One of his cousins, Jacob Berlin (son of John D. Berlin, an uncle, one of the Berlins who lived in Indiana), "was killed at the siege of Vicksburg." Berlin's memorandum on his family was not a history of the family's participation in American history, although the westward migration of many of his relatives and the eventual separation of the generations and the cousins by hundreds and thousands of miles was one of the most important of all the dramas of the American history through which they all lived.

"This leaves myself alone to account for," Berlin concluded. "I married Susan M. Holt of Augusta County, Va. ten days after I left Judge Thompsons Law School at Staunton Va. March 31st. 1846, and have practiced law ever since, 15 years in Upshur and adjoining Counties in W. Va. and here (Harrisonburg Va.) ever since." He named each of his five living sons and two living daughters, but he did not chose to name the daughter and son who had died in infancy, and he wrote no more about their mother, about his wife whom he always called Sue. As of the time that he prepared the memorandum, Berlin yet had no grandchildren to enumerate, to convey the family history to, to warn against bad men, as he had warned Lee and Mary in that letter in March 1861. There would be grandchildren later, but not then. When he wrote his family history memorandum and recorded who had lived where and who had moved away, only he and two sons were living in Bridgewater. One of his daughters was married and in New York, and one was away attending school.

It was a very different world in which Berlin wrote about his family, different in many material and immaterial ways from the world of 1861. The old South was gone forever and slavery with it, permanently altering relationships between white people and black people, between people with property and people without, between people who worked for themselves and people who worked for others. All the old relationships based on slavery were gone. Virginia, like the nation, had been split in two but, unlike the nation, had not reunited afterward. Virginia became the primary eastern battleground of the war, which spread its desolation nearly everywhere. Old Virginia was the most conspicuous victim of the war. The only thing that Virginia gained from the war was the abolition of slavery, and for George Berlin and many other white Virginians of his generation, they did not at that time initially regard abolition as a good thing.

The meager surviving family records of the period between George and Susan's reunion in 1862 and his death in 1895 contain few clues about George Berlin's visceral reactions to all of the changes. He might list Thaddeus Stevens and Benjamin F. Butler in his catalog of historical villains (nearly all white Southerners did that for generations), but it is not clear how he adjusted to the new realities or whether he longed for that which was lost. Like most people, he probably did the best that he could with the lot that fell to him after the war ended and after his wife died.

George Berlin's life after the war was not the life that he and Susan had dreamed about and had tried to create during the fifteen years that they lived together in Randolph and Upshur Counties, nor was it the life that they had dreamed about and tried to create during the four and a half years that they lived together in Augusta and Rockingham Counties. Inexorable change had carried him and his family along with it. He had played his little part in a great national drama and had suffered some of the consequences of a war that he could not prevent. He had lost his law practice and property in western Virginia, he had lost his wife, and his extended family had dispersed after he moved back to eastern Virginia. Some of those personal losses could be directly attributed to the war, some to the march of time.

The long view of history presents a different picture than when one is caught up in its unfolding events. Precisely what George Berlin thought when he looked back late in life is not easy to know, but he could never ignore how much had changed during that time and in part as a consequence of the Civil War that began with his participation in the Convention of 1861 and that brought about the two long separations from his wife. Gray hair would have been only one of the outward manifestations of the passage of time or the pressures of the times.

George William Berlin died at his home in Bridgewater on November 13, 1895, probably of pneumonia that may have afflicted his lungs

Gravestone of George and Susan Berlin in Woodbine Cemetery, Harrisonburg. (Photograph by the author)

as a consequence of a weakened heart. He was buried beside the body of Susan Berlin in Harrisonburg's Woodbine Cemetery, reunited, after their longest separation, for the last time.

The two local newspapers, the *Bridgewater Herald* and Harrisonburg's *Rockingham Recorder*, printed obituaries that outlined his career and reported on his marriage, the births of his children, and the death of his wife. Berlin's youngest son, George Richard, was editor of the *Herald*, and he modestly allowed the editor of the *Recorder* to eulogize his father, but he quoted the *Recorder* eulogy at length.[8] Berlin would no doubt have been pleased at some of the things that the author of the obituary in the *Rockingham Recorder* especially noted. He wrote of Berlin: "In his manner he was dignified without brusqueness, and was companionable and interesting without being effusive. He was a type of the old school, deliberate in thought, firmly set in his convictions, but always considerate of the opinions of others." That is exactly how Berlin wanted to be perceived. The writer also remembered another thing about Berlin that was often noted and of which he was always proud: his careful preparation, that he was "methodical and painstaking to the last degree. As a lawyer he displayed tenacity of purpose and the greatest industry in the preparation of his cases."

And one more thing. It was almost thirty-five years since the secession crisis and Berlin's service in the state convention and all of its painful consequences. The editor of the *Rockingham Recorder* knew and remembered that connection between the personal history of George Berlin and the dramatic national history, and he thought it proper to remind his readers of that fact, that his readers should know that this man, George W. Berlin, had been there and had taken part in that event of great importance, the secession of Virginia. The editor wrote of George W. Berlin that he had been a member of the Convention in 1861 and "though elected as a Union man, he finally consented to sign the ordinance of secession—an act for which he frequently expressed regret in later years."[9]

Notes

ABBREVIATIONS AND SHORT TITLES

BMFP   Berlin-Martz Family Papers, Acc. 36271, Library of Virginia, Richmond
GWB   George William Berlin
Proceedings   George H. Reese and William H. Gaines, eds., *Proceedings of the Virginia State Convention of 1861*, 4 vols. (Richmond, 1965)
SMHB   Susan Miranda Holt Berlin

1 DAYDREAMS

1. John Tyler, full text in *Proceedings* 1:636–54, 660–81.

2. Daphne Gentry, "Berlin, George William," in John T. Kneebone et al., eds., *Dictionary of Virginia Biography* (Richmond, 1998–), 1:458–59.

3. Children then living identified in United States Census, Upshur Co., Va., 1860, and in his obituary in the *Harrisonburg (Va.) Rockingham Recorder*, Nov. 15, 1895, clipping in BMFP, the source for all letters hereafter cited unless otherwise stated.

4. GWB to SMHB, Mar. 14, 1861.

5. SMHB to GWB, Feb. 27, and 29 [*sic*], 1861, and GWB to SMHB, Mar. 3, 1861.

6. GWB to SMHB, Feb. 21, 1861.

7. GWB to SMHB, June 3, 1852.

8. Account of the fire in *Cooper's Clarksburg (Va.) Register*, Nov. 7, 1855, does not mention destruction of, or damage to, Berlin's house, although his law office and the house of his brother, Frederick Berlin, are listed among the buildings burned; work on the house mentioned in GWB to SMHB, May 27, 1856.

9. E.g., Beth Barton Schweiger, *The Gospel Working Up: Progress and the Pulpit in Nineteenth Century Virginia* (New York, 2000); Ami Pflugrad-Jackisch, *Brothers of a Vow: Secret Fraternal Orders and the Transformation of White Male Culture in Antebellum Virginia* (Athens, Ga.: 2010); Jonathan Daniel Wells and Jennifer R. Green, eds., *The Southern Middle Class in the Long Nineteenth Century* (Baton Rouge, La., 2011).

10. Brent Tarter, *The Grandees of Government: The Origins and Persistence of Undemocratic Politics in Virginia* (Charlottesville, Va., 2013), 189, 203.

11. Frederick Berlin to Emory Lee Berlin, Nov. 24, 1895.

12. GWB to Frederick Berlin, Jan. 22, 1844.

13. On Sept. 1, 1844, *Second Marriage Record of Augusta County, Va. 1813–50* (Staunton, Va., 1972), 84.

14. GWB's undated family history memorandum, BMFP; GWB to SMHB, Mar. 31, 1861; marriage not listed in Augusta Co. Marriage Record.

15. Licenses, dated Feb. 23, Mar. 12, 1846, BMFP.

16. GWB to SMHB, several letters dated at Beverly between Aug. 2, 1847, and May 28, 1849; United States Census, Lewis Co., Va., 1860.

17. GWB to SMHB, June 3, 1852.

18. Frances W. Saunders, "Equestrian Washington: From Rome to Richmond," *Virginia Cavalcade* 25 (1975): 4–13; Elizabeth R. Varon, "'The Ladies Are Whigs': Lucy Barbour, Henry Clay, and Nineteenth-Century Virginia Politics," *Virginia Cavalcade* 42 (1992): 72–83.

19. GWB to SMHB, June 2, 1852.

20. United States Census, 1860, Upshur Co., Va.

21. GWB to SMHB, Feb. 11, 14, 1861.

22. GWB to SMHB, Feb. 11, 1861.

23. Ibid.

24. GWB to SMHB, Mar. 28, 1861; memorandum of appointment, Mar. 26, 1861, Executive Papers of Governor John Letcher, Record Group 3, Library of Virginia.

25. F. N. Boney, *John Letcher of Virginia: The Story of Virginia's Civil War Governor* (University, Ala., 1966), 27, 32.

26. GWB to Lee and Mary, Mar. 14–15, 1861.

27. GWB to SMHB, Feb. 11, 14, 26, 1861.

28. SMHB to GWB, Mar. 27, 1861; GWB to SMHB, Mar. 4, 1861.

29. GWB to SMHB, Feb. 14, 1861.

30. GWB to Frederick Berlin, Jan. 22, 1846; GWB to SMHB, June 2, 1852.

31. Upshur Co. presidential election polls, 1852, Election Records, Secretary of the Commonwealth, Record Group 13, Acc. 38055, Library of Virginia.

32. *Cooper's Clarksburg Register*, Nov. 17, 1852.

33. *Cooper's Clarksburg Register*, June 19, 1857.

34. Boney, *John Letcher*, 74–90; William A. Link, *Roots of Secession: Slavery and Politics in Antebellum Virginia* (Chapel Hill, N.C., 2003), 121–48; *Cooper's Clarksburg Register*, June 5, 1857, reporting 1857 congressional returns and contrasting them with 1855 returns; *Richmond Daily Whig*, Nov. 6, 1860, reporting Democratic victory margin in Upshur Co. of 130 in 1859.

35. *Cooper's Clarksburg Register,* Nov. 21, 1856; W. B. Cutright, *The History of Upshur County, West Virginia, from its Earliest Exploration and Settlement to the Present Time* (Buckhannon, W.Va., 1907), 296–99. There is no official election return from Upshur Co. listing voters and how they voted for the 1856 presidential election in the Secretary of the Commonwealth records.

36. Richard L. Brown to GWB, Oct. 5, 1860, Richard L. Brown Papers, Acc. 38759, Library of Virginia; *Cooper's Clarksburg Register,* Nov. 21, 1856.

37. Upshur Co. 1860 presidential election return, Election Records, Secretary of the Commonwealth, Record Group 13, Acc. 38055, *Richmond Daily Dispatch,* Dec. 24, 1860; Tarter, *Grandees of Government,* 198–201.

38. Diary of Henry F. Westfall, Jan. 17, 29, 1861, Upshur Co. Historical Society, Buckhannon, W.Va.; typed transcription also in library of West Virginia University, Morganton, W.Va.

39. Diary of Henry F. Westfall, Jan. 20, 21, 1861.

40. BMFP.

41. Elizabeth R. Varon, *Disunion! The Coming of the American Civil War, 1789–1859* (Chapel Hill, N.C., 2008).

42. Diary of Henry F. Westfall, Feb. 4, 1861.

43. Voters in Upshur County at the May 23, 1861, referendum on secession voted in at least two places, as indicated by incomplete surviving poll books, Upshur Co. Historical Society.

44. Tarter, *Grandees of Government,* 202.

45. Ibid., 197–206.

46. Daniel W. Crofts, *Reluctant Confederates: Upper South Unionists in the Secession Crisis* (Chapel Hill, N.C., 1989); Tarter, *Grandees of Government,* 197.

47. United States Census, Slave Schedule, Upshur Co., Va., 1860; Personal Property Tax Returns, Upshur Co., Va., 1860, Auditor of Public Accounts, Record Group 48, Library of Virginia.

48. United States Census, Slave Schedule, Barbour Co., Va., 1860.

49. United States Census, Slave Schedule, Upshur Co., Va., 1860; United States Census, Upshur Co., Va., 1860.

50. Wilma A. Dunaway, *Slavery in the American Mountain South* (Cambridge, England, 2003).

51. GWB to SMHB, May 27, 1856.

52. GWB to SMHB, Oct. 18, 1854.

53. Ibid.

54. John Zaborney, *Slaves for Hire: Renting Enslaved Laborers in Antebellum Virginia* (Baton Rouge, La., 2012).

55. SMHB to GWB, Feb. 29 [*sic*], Mar. 6, 1861.

56. GWB to SMHB, Mar. 14, 1861.

57. GWB to SMHB, Apr. 7, 1861.

58. Upshur Co. Land Tax Return, 1860, Record Group 48, Library of Virginia.

59. GWB to SMHB, July 4, 1849.

60. GWB to SMHB, Mar. 25, 1861.

61. SMHB to GWB, Mar. 27, 1861.

62. GWB to SMHB, Mar. 29, 1861.

63. SMHB to GWB, Mar. 18, 27, 1861.

64. GWB to SMHB, Mar. 22, 1861.

65. Huldah W. Holt, age fifteen, married John Diddle, age twenty-two (Augusta Co. Marriage Register, Sept. 14, 1855).

66. George W. Diddle, age fourteen, is listed on the 1870 census of Barbour Co., W.Va., residing with his grandfather, Thomas Holt, who in that same year mentioned him in Thomas Holt to GWB, Oct. 2, 1870.

67. The 1860 Census, Upshur Co., Va., listed John Dean Jr., age twenty-seven, wife Hulda, age twenty-three, daughter Isadora, age three and an unnamed daughter, age four months. The census enumerator left empty the blank for Dean's aggregate wealth but entered the sum of $130 opposite Hulda's name. The county personal property tax list (Auditor of Public Accounts, Record Group 48, Library of Virginia) also lists John Dean Jr. and indicates that he owned a slave but does not list any other taxable property, not even the two calves Hulda is known to have owned. The two records are so inconsistent with each other that it is not clear which data in each may be correct or even whether either refers to the family of Susan Berlin's sister.

68. GWB to SMHB, Mar. 22, 1861.

69. Daughter Alice mentioned in GWB to SMHB, Aug. 2, 1847; "the memory of our *Dear little Alice*" in GWB to SMHB, May 28, 1849.

70. Born in May 1852, named later, identified in later dockets on GWB to SMHB, May 7, 18, June 21, 1852.

71. GWB to SMHB, Mar. 31, 1861.

72. GWB to SMHB, Jan. 15, 1862.

73. GWB to SMHB, Oct. 30, 1854.

74. SMHB to GWB, Feb. 27, 1861.

75. GWB to SMHB, Mar. 4, 1861; SMHB to GWB, Mar. 10, 1861.

76. SMHB to GWB, Mar. 10, 1861.

2 Speech

1. *Proceedings* 1:197.

2. Ibid., 1:50–75, 76–93; Charles B. Dew, *Apostles of Disunion: Southern Secession Commissioners and the Causes of the Civil War* (Charlottesville, Va., 2001), 59–73.

134 | NOTES TO PAGES 26–35

3. GWB to SMHB, June 27, 1852; *Rockingham Register*, Nov. 15, 1895, copy in BMFP.

4. Undated draft speech, BMFP.

5. GWB to SMHB, Apr. 10, 1861.

6. Charles Henry Ambler, *Sectionalism in Virginia from 1776 to 1861* (Chicago, 1910); Tarter, *Grandees of Government*, 176–81, 185–93, 203–6, 211–16.

7. *Cooper's Clarksburg Register*, Nov. 7, 1855.

8. John E. Stealey III, *West Virginia's Civil War-Era Constitution: Loyal Revolution, Confederate Counter-Revolution, and the Convention of 1872* (Kent, Ohio, 2013), 32–71; Tarter, *Grandees of Government*, 191–92, 213–16.

3 NIGHTMARES

1. Tarter, *Grandees of Government*, 209, 420.

2. GWB to SMHB, Apr. 7, 1861.

3. GWB to SMHB, June 27, 1852.

4. SMHB to GWB, Mar. 10, 1861.

5. GWB to SMHB, Apr. 10, 1861.

6. GWB to SMHB, Mar. 17, 1861.

7. SMHB to GWB, Feb. 29 [*sic*], 1861.

8. Ibid.

9. SMHB to GWB, Apr. 5, 1861.

10. SMHB to GWB, Feb. 29 [*sic*], 1861.

11. SMHB to GWB, Mar. 18, 1861.

12. Ibid.

13. SMHB to GWB, Mar. 6, 10, 18, Apr. 5, 1861; Diary of Henry F. Westfall, Apr. 8, 9, 10, 11, 12, 1861.

14. SMHB to GWB, Apr. 5, 1861.

15. SMHB to GWB, Mar. 18, 1861.

16. GWB to SMHB, Mar. 22, 1861.

17. SMHB to GWB, Mar. 18, 1861.

18. GWB to SMHB, 22 Mar. 1861.

19. SMHB to GWB, Mar. 10, 1861.

20. SMHB to GWB, Sept. 20, 1861.

21. SMHB to GWB, Mar. 27, 1861.

22. Ibid.

23. Ruth Woods Dayton, ed., *Samuel Woods and His Family* (Charleston, W.Va., 1939), 1–2.

24. GWB to SMHB, Apr. 13–14, 1861.

25. GWB to SMHB, Apr. 12, 1861.

26. SMHB to GWB, Apr. 22, 1861.

4 Secession

1. GWB to SMHB, Apr. 13–14, 1861.

2. *Proceedings* 4:26–27.

3. *Proceedings* 4:52–54; William W. Freehling, "Virginia's Reluctant Secession," *North & South* 5 (May 2002): 80–89; Tarter, *Grandees of Government*, 210–13.

4. Craig M. Simpson, *A Good Southerner: The Life of Henry A. Wise of Virginia* (Chapel Hill, N.C., 1985), 250.

5. *Proceedings* 4:52–54.

6. GWB to SMHB, Apr. 19, 1861.

7. SMHB to GWB, Apr. 22, 1861.

8. *Proceedings* 4:401–2.

9. Ibid., 4:403–5.

10. GWB to SMHB, Apr. 25, 1861.

11. Diary of Henry F. Westfall, Apr. 29, 1861.

12. Notes of last speech made in Buckhannon, BMFP.

13. Undated slip of paper initialed "M. E. L." (Mary E. Berlin Latham), BMFP.

5 Separation

1. John W. Shaffer, *Clash of Loyalties: A Border County in the Civil War* (Morgantown, W.Va., 2003), esp. 15, 49–67, emphasizing these strains in neighboring Barbour County.

2. David L. Phillips and Rebecca L. Hill, *War Stories: Civil War in West Virginia* (Leesburg, Va., 1991); Kenneth W. Noe and Shannon H. Wilson, eds., *The Civil War in Appalachia: Collected Essays* (Knoxville, Tenn., 1997).

3. Diary of Henry F. Westfall, May 17, 1861. Two polls, one an original, one a photocopy, Upshur Co. Historical Society, Buckhannon, W. Va.

4. Cutright, *History of Upshur County*, 300; Betty Hornbeck, *Upshur Boys in Blue and Gray* (Parson, W.Va., 1967), 16.

5. Diary of Henry F. Westfall, Mar. 29, Apr. 8, 9, 10, 11, 12, May 1, 2, 8, 24, June 12, 14, 22, 23, 1861.

6. GWB to James A. Seddon, Apr. 24, 1863.

7. GWB to SMHB, June 15, 1861.

8. Ibid.

9. GWB to SMHB, June 17, 1861.

10. George H. Reese, ed., *Journals and Papers of the Virginia State Convention of 1861*, 3 vols. (Richmond, 1966), 1:306–15.

11. *Proceedings* 4:545.

12. Tarter, *Grandees of Government*, 216.

13. GWB Letters from Beverley to SMHB, Feb. 12, 1846, Aug. 2, 15, 1847, Apr. 8, 25, 1849, May 12, 18, 1849.

14. *The War of the Rebellion: A Compilation of the Official Records of the Union and Confederate Armies*, series 1, 2 (Washington, D.C., 1880): 279, 281.

15. *My Poor Dear Syl . . . The Upshur County Civil War Diary and Letters of Marcia Louise Sumner Phillips* (Buckhannon, W.Va., 2013), 3.

16. Ibid., 4.

17. SMHB to GWB, July 5, 1861.

18. Dayton, *Samuel Woods and His Family*, 36.

19. SMHB to GWB, July 5, 1861.

20. Diary of Henry F. Westfall, July 22, 1861; GWB to James A. Seddon, Apr. 24, 1863.

21. *My Poor Dear Syl*, 74.

22. Ibid., 12, 13.

23. Ibid., 16–18.

24. SMHB to GWB, July 5, 1861.

25. John Beatty, *The Citizen-Soldier; or, Memoirs of a Volunteer* (Cincinnati, Ohio, 1879), 13–14.

26. George B. McClellan to J. D. Cox, July 2, 1861, in *The War of the Rebellion*, series 1, 2: 197.

27. SMHB to GWB, July 5, 1861.

28. George B. McClellan to E. D. Townsend, July 5, 1861, in *The War of the Rebellion*, series 1, 2: 198.

29. Beatty, *Citizen-Soldier*, 31.

30. Crofts, *Reluctant Confederates*, 117–22.

31. Beatty, *Citizen-Soldier*, 16.

32. Charles Richard Williams, ed., *Diary and Letters of Rutherford Birchard Hayes, Nineteenth President of the United States*, 5 vols. (Columbus, Ohio, 1922–26), 2:49.

33. Ibid., 2:64.

34. Ibid., 2:68, 69; Shaffer, *Clash of Loyalties*, 81–104.

35. Isabella Neeson Woods to Samuel Woods, Sept. 5, 1861, in Dayton, *Samuel Woods and His Family*, 36.

36. SMHB to GWB, July 5, 1861.

37. SMHB to GWB, July 5, Oct. 27, 1861.

38. SMHB to GWB, July 15, 1861.

39. GWB to SMHB, June 15, 1861.

40. SMHB to GWB, July 15, 1861.

41. Diary of Henry F. Westfall, Aug. 4, 1861.

42. SMHB to GWB, Sept. 4, 1861.

43. SMHB to GWB, July 15, 1861.

44. SMHB to GWB, 15 July 1861.

45. SMHB to GWB, Sept. 4, 1861.

46. SMHB to GWB, Sept. 26, 1861.

47. No piano is listed in the Upshur Co. Personal Property Tax Return, 1860, although pianos were taxable personal property, but the piano may have been at Frederick and Maria Berlin's house at the time of the tax assessment, as it was at the time of the flood.

48. SMHB to GWB, Sept. 26, 1861; Hu Maxwell, *History of Barbour County, West Virginia, from Its Earliest Exploration and Settlement to the Present Time* (Morgantown, W.Va., 1899), 210–11, 481–82.

49. SMHB to GWB, Sept. 26, 1861.

50. Ibid.

51. United States Census, Slave Schedule, Barbour Co., Va., 1860.

52. Isabella Neeson Woods to Samuel Woods, Sept. 16, Oct. 8, 1861, in Dayton, *Samuel Woods and His Family*, 37, 47.

53. SMHB to GWB, dated "Buchanan Oct 6th Sept. 26th 1861."

54. Isabella Neeson Woods to Samuel Woods, Sept. 16, 1861, in Dayton, *Samuel Woods and His Family*, 36.

55. SMHB to GWB, dated "Buchanan Oct 6th Sept. 26th 1861."

56. Ibid.

57. SMHB to GWB, Oct. 27, 1861.

58. SMHB to GWB, Jan. 3, 1862.

59. SMHB to GWB, dated "Buchanan Oct 6th Sept. 26th 1861."

60. SMHB to GWB, Oct. 27, 1861.

61. Ibid.

62. SMHB to GWB, Jan. 3, 1862.

63. SMHB to GWB, Oct. 27, 1861.

64. Joan E. Cashin, "The Refugee Experience in the Civil War," in *A Woman's War: Southern Women, Civil War, and the Confederate Legacy*, ed. Edward D. C. Campbell Jr. and Kym S. Rice (Richmond, 1996), 29–54, 195–22; Amy Murrell Taylor, *The Divided Family in Civil War America* (Chapel Hill, N.C., 2005); Shaffer, *Clash of Loyalties*, 105–28.

65. SMHB to GWB, Jan. 3, 1865.

66. *My Poor Dear Syl*, 64–65.

67. Ibid., 66.

68. Ibid., 70.

69. SMHB to GWB, Oct., 1861; *My Poor Dear Syl*, 47; undated list of fifteen Upshur County men that GWB prepared, ca. Feb. 1861 (BMFP), to receive free copies of the *Richmond Enquirer* that printed the convention's debates during the continuance of the convention.

70. *My Poor Dear Syl*, 71.

71. Diary of Henry F. Westfall, notes on Apr. 2, 1862, referendum, p. 130.

72. Hornbeck, *Upshur Brothers of the Blue and Gray*, 155–248.

73. Cutright, *History of Upshur County*, 280–81.

74. *My Poor Dear Syl*, 71.

75. Ibid., 72.

76. Ibid., 46.

77. Ibid., 72.

78. SMHB to GWB, Jan. 3, 1862.

79. Isabella Neeson Woods to Samuel Woods, Jan. 3, 1862, in Dayton, *Samuel Woods and His Family*, 62.

80. GWB to SMHB, Jan. 15, 1862.

81. Ibid.; his letter to Frederick Berlin is not in the family files.

82. GWB to SMHB, Jan. 15, 1862.

83. GWB to SMHB, Mar. 28, 1862.

84. GWB to Robert E. Lee, Aug. 10, 1861.

85. Thomas Holt to GWB, Oct. 20, 1861; Augusta County Deed Book 80 (1860–63), 508; Isabella Neeson Woods to Samuel Woods, Jan. 3, 1862, in Dayton, *Samuel Woods and His Family*, 62; Diary of Henry F. Westfall, Dec. 27, 28, 1861, Jan. 2, 3, 4, 1862.

86. GWB to SMHB, Mar. 31, 1862.

87. GWB to SMHB, Mar. 28, 1862.

88. GWB to SMHB, Mar. 31, 1862.

89. *My Poor Dear Syl*, 74; Isabella Neeson Woods to Samuel Woods, Feb. 19, 1862, in Dayton, *Samuel Woods and His Family*, 68.

90. Shaffer, *Clash of Loyalties*, 14.

91. GWB to SMHB, Mar. 31, 1862; SMHB to GWB, Oct. 27, 1861.

92. Shaffer, *Clash of Loyalties*, 129–48.

93. SMHB to GWB, Apr. 22, 1861.

94. GWB to SMHB, Apr. 20, 1862.

95. Ibid.

96. "Letter written in vindication of West Va. in 1862," BMFP.

97. Undated draft essay, "Written upon the encroachment of Abolition," BMFP.

98. Undated draft essay on the topic of guerilla war, BMFP.

6 REUNION

1. Isabella Neeson Woods to Samuel Woods, June 18, 1862, in Dayton, *Samuel Woods and His Family*, 74.

2. SMHB to GWB, June 22, 1862.

3. SMHB to GWB, July 14, 1862.

4. SMHB to GWB, Feb. 29 [*sic*], 1862.

5. SMHB to GWB, Mar. 27, 1861.

6. GWB to SMHB, Mar. 31, 1862.

7. United States Census, Upshur Co., Va., 1860.

8. *150 Years in Review: The Buckhannon Presbyterian Church, 1849–1999* (n.p., 1999), 2, 67.

9. Gentry, "Berlin, George William," 1:458.

10. Diary of Henry F. Westfall, Jan. 26, Feb. 10, 1861.

11. Howard McKnight Wilson, *The Lexington Presbytery Heritage: The Presbytery of Lexington and Its Churches in the Synod of Virginia, Presbyterian Church in the United States* (Verona, Va., 1971), 378, 388.

12. GWB to SMHB, Aug. 23, 1862.

13. Ibid.

14. Ibid.

15. SMHB to GWB, Sept. 19, 1862.

16. GWB to James A. Seddon, Aug. 24, 1863.

17. Ibid.; Hugh W. Sheffey to James A. Seddon, Aug. 28, 1863, John Letcher to James A. Seddon, Sept. 9, 1863, and order of Orlando Smith, Sept. 4, 1863, William Smith to GWB, Apr. 8, 1864.

18. Attested affidavit of William Smith, Apr. 28, 1864.

19. *Bridgewater (Va.) Herald*, Nov. 15, 1895, copy in BMFP; surviving company records contain few documents from that period (Staunton and Parkersburg Turnpike Company Records, Board of Public Works Papers, Record Group 57, Library of Virginia).

20. Richard L. Brown to GWB, Feb. 6, 1863, Richard L. Brown Papers, Library of Virginia.

21. Oaths of allegiance, May 26, and June 21, 1861, BMFP.

22. Thomas Holt to GWB, Oct. 2, 1870.

23. Thomas Holt to GWB, May 28, 1868.

24. Odie Velta Nestor Chapman, *They Rest Quietly: Cemetery Records of Barbour County, West Virginia* (Parsons, W.Va., 1999), 193.

25. Ibid., 192.

26. *Rockingham Register*, Nov. 15, 1895, copy, and manuscript funeral notice, both in BMFP.

7 Regrets

1. C. E. May, *Life under Four Flags in the North River Basin of Virginia* (Verona, Va., 1976), 453–55.

2. "Pure Bone-Dust For Sale," undated broadside, and *Rockingham Advertiser*, Aug. 16, 1880, both in BMFP.

3. Several letters to GWB from his children, addressed to him in Buckhannon, in 1874, BMFP; copy of will of Thomas Holt, dated July 2, 1870, proved Sept. 28, 1872, BMFP.

4. Mary Stemple Coffman, *Barbour County, West Virginia: Book of Deaths 1, 1853–1919 and Will Books 1 and 1½, 1839–1899* (Bowie, Md., 1994), 118.

5. United States Census, 1880, Barbour Co., W. Va.; Coffman, *Barbour County, West Virginia: Book of Deaths*, 213.

6. Undated and untitled draft essay, BMFP.

7. Undated and untitled manuscript, Berlin family history, ca. 1880s, BMFP.

8. *Bridgewater Herald*, Nov. 15, 1895, BMFP.

9. Ibid.

Index

GWB and SMHB denote George William Berlin and Susan Miranda Holt Berlin, respectively, and italicized page numbers refer to illustrations.

Holt, William F. (Will or Ferd; brother of SMHB), 96, 97, 122
Holt family, 64, 125
Hughes, John N., 92

Jackson, John Jay, 36
James River and Kanawha Canal, 46
Janney, John, 36
Jefferson, Thomas, 36

Lebanon White Sulphur Spring Hotel, 118
Lee, Robert E., 76, 105, 107
Leslie's Illustrated Weekly, 15
Letcher, John, 14, 19, 70–71
Letcher, Susan Holt (cousin of SMHB), 14
Lincoln, Abraham, 13, 51, 59, 67–68, 81, 86, 95; calls for troops, 71, 75, 76, 81, 85; election of, 2, 19, 20, 22, 24, 43, 58
Lynchburg, 44, 46

McClellan, George B., 94–95
Middlebrook, 120
Milt (aka Mit, Milton; enslaved man), 64, 99, 102
Missouri Compromise, 10, 40
Monterey, 89, 93, 107, 110, 111
Moore, Samuel McDowell, 36

Norfolk, 75, 81
nullification crisis, 40, 51

Passmore, Lewis, 126
Peace Conference (1861), 1–2, 13, 14, 34, 49, 81, 82
personal liberty laws, 42, 83
petroleum/oil, 13–14, 31
Philippi, 15, 29, 31, 64–65, 66, 89, 93, 96, 98, 109, 113, 114, 115, 118, 119, 121, 122
"Philippi Races," 89

Phillips, Marcia Louise Sumner, 93–94, 103, 104–5, 109
Phillips, Sylvester B., 103, 104–5
Pickens, Francis, 81, 83
Pierce, Franklin, 18
Portsmouth, 81, 83
Powhatan House, 16, 39, 72

railroads, 41, 43–46, 47, 48, 73, 74, 123, 126
Randolph, George Wythe, 36
Randolph County, 92–93, 96, 128
refugees from western Virginia, 110, 111
Reger, Albert, 88
Reger, John W., 88
religion, 115–18
Republican Party, 19–20, 43, 51–52, 95, 104
Richmond, 1, 5, 14–17, 24, 29, 39, 70–71; Capitol Square, 11–12, 16–17; Mechanics Institute, 2, 37. *See also* Virginia Convention
Rockingham County, 121, 128
Rockingham Recorder, 129–30

Scott, Winfield, 18
secession, 1, 3; GWB condemns, 21–24, 34–53, 72–75; GWB endorses, 76–78, 79–85, 88, 107; opponents of, 36–39, 57–58, 71–72; referendum on, 23–24, 85, 87–88; SMHB endorses, 97, 98, 100–101, 103, 104–5; supporters of, 34–35, 37, 58–59, 70–71, 93; Virginia Convention votes on, 54, 72; Virginia ordinance of, *90,* 91–92, 130
sectionalism, 12, 21, 53; in Virginia, 39–41, 44–50
servants, 26, 61–62, 64, 103
slavery, 1–2, 34–35, 42, 58–59, 74, 82, 112; gaining freedom from, 98–99, 100, 102, 127–28; GWB approves, 21–22, 24–28,

Recent Books in the Series

A NATION DIVIDED: STUDIES IN THE CIVIL WAR ERA